The Gospel According
to Tolkien

The Gospel According to Tolkien

Visions of the Kingdom in Middle-earth

Ralph C. Wood

WESTMINSTER
JOHN KNOX PRESS
LOUISVILLE · KENTUCKY

Scripture quotations from the Revised Standard Version of the Bible are copyright © 1946, 1952, 1971, and 1973 by the Division of Christian Education of the National Council of the Churches of Christ in the U.S.A. and are used by permission.

See acknowledgments, pp. 168–69, for additional permission information.

Book design by Sharon Adams
Cover design by Jennifer K. Cox

First edition
Published by Westminster John Knox Press
Louisville, Kentucky

This book is printed on acid-free paper that meets the American National Standards Institute Z39.48 standard. ⊗

11 12 — 10 9 8 7 6 5 4 3

Library of Congress Cataloging-in-Publication Data

Wood, Ralph C.
     The gospel according to Tolkien : visions of the kingdom in middle-earth / Ralph C. Wood.—1st ed.
         p. cm.
     ISBN 0-664-22610-8 (alk. paper)
     1. Tolkien, J. R. R. (John Ronald Reuel), 1892–1973. Lord of the rings. 2. Tolkien, J. R. R. (John Ronald Reuel), 1892–1973—Religion. 3. Christianity and literature—England—History—20th century. 4. Christian fiction, English—History and criticism. 5. Fantasy fiction, English—History and criticism. 6. Christian ethics in literature. 7. Middle Earth (Imaginary place) I. Title.

PR6039.O32L63 2003
823'.912—dc21

2003047901

For John Sykes
my student, friend, and companion in the Quest

Contents

Preface   ix

Introduction   1

1 The Great Symphony of the Creation   11

2 The Calamity of Evil: The Marring of the Divine Harmony   48

3 The Counter-Action to Evil: Tolkien's Vision of the Moral Life   75

4 The Lasting Corrective: Tolkien's Vision of the Redeemed Life   117

5 Consummation: When Middle-earth Shall Be Unmarred   156

Bibliography   166

Acknowledgments   168

Preface

*T*his theological meditation on *The Lord of the Rings* does not enter into the many debates among scholars about the various and often conflicting interpretations of Tolkien. I seek nothing more or less than to make the Christian dimension of this great book accessible to the ordinary interested reader of Tolkien. Yet the absence of footnotes hardly means that the author owes no debts. Quite to the contrary, I am immensely grateful to the many Tolkien scholars whose work I have silently drawn from. My treatment of the classical virtues will reveal my obvious reliance on Josef Pieper's classic little treatise, *The Four Cardinal Virtues*, even as my estimate of the theological virtues, especially charity understood as forgiveness, will disclose my continuing homage to the work of Karl Barth. Paul J. Wadell's *Friendship and the Moral Life* has also been indispensable for my thinking about the place of *philia* in the life of the Fellowship.

The parenthetical citations refer to the standard cloth-bound editions of major works by and about Tolkien, with the following abbreviations: *The Hobbit* (H), *The Letters of J. R. R. Tolkien* (L), *The Silmarillion* (S), *"The Monsters and the Critics" and Other Essays* (MC), *Morgoth's Ring* (MR), *The Peoples of Middle-earth* (PM), *Smith of Wootton Major* (SWM), and Humphrey Carpenter's *Tolkien: A Biography* (T). *The Lord of the Rings* itself will be paginated according to the three separate volumes—1: *The Fellowship of the Ring*, 2: *The Two Towers*, and 3: *The Return of the King*. All quotations from the Bible are taken from the Revised Standard Version, since it retains the thee-you distinction that was important to Tolkien. I have employed, again in faithfulness to

Tolkien's undeviating practice, his use of "man" and "men" to refer to our common humanity. I have also followed his practice of liberally capitalizing many nouns that are often put in the lower case. This is not only a way of honoring the deeply Germanic bent of his work but also of acknowledging his more important concern—not to flatten everything into a bland egalitarian sameness, but rather to exalt matters that truly deserve the upper case.

Clandestine readers of *The Lord of the Rings* behind the Iron Curtain, where it was strictly forbidden, were called Tolkienisti. I owe immeasurable gratitude to my many friends who are fellow Tolkienisti: Mike Beaty, Kyle Childress, Bill Crow, Barry Harvey, Russ Hightower, Christopher Mitchell, Scott Moore, Byron Newberry, Mark Noll, Robin Reid, David and Jeanie Ryden, Adam Schwartz, Gray Smith, Timothy Vaverek, and Robb Wilson. I want also to commend several youngsters who, already as passionate about *The Lord of the Rings* as their parents, represent the new generation of Tolkien readers and future scholars: Joshua and Gideon, the sons of Katherine and David Jeffrey; Kristen, Rob, and Brandon, the children of Cheryl and Richard Myrick; Timothy and Andrew, the sons of Wanda and Gray Smith; Nathaniel and Andrew, the sons of Jennifer and Christopher Eberlein; Brittany, Gerad, James, and Diana, the children of Michelle and Glenn Gentry. I owe an especially large debt to my graduate assistant, Don Shipley, to my student Paula Fluhrer, and to my dear wife, Suzanne. They have read the manuscript and checked all the quotations with painstaking and mind-numbing literalism. Five of my Baylor students and colleagues—Ben Johnson, Helen Lasseter, Mark Long, Elisabeth Wolfe, and Randy Woodruff—have all read my manuscript-in-progress with immense care. Not only have they saved me from many factual errors; they have also corrected many misinterpretations, often supplying accurate ones in their stead. I have shamelessly raided their ideas and insights.

My thanksgiving would not be complete without offering gratitude to the many audiences, both academic and ecclesial, who have listened to my lectures and engaged me in lively discussion of Tolkien's work. Here I can do no more than list the churches and schools that have received me with extraordinary kindness: Mount

Tabor United Methodist in Winston-Salem, Park Cities Presbyterian in Dallas, Saint Charles Avenue Baptist in New Orleans, Saint Alban's Episcopal in Waco, Calvin College, the Cambridge School of Dallas, Cleveland State University, the Duke University Divinity School, Louisiana State University–Baton Rouge, Louisiana State University–Shreveport, the University of Notre Dame, Oberlin College, the University of Oklahoma, Oklahoma State University, Southern Methodist University, Texas A&M University–College Station, Texas A&M University–Commerce, and the Texas Military Institute. There is not space to list the scores of students from whom I learned much about Tolkien during the years 1986–97, when they took my course called "Faith and Imagination" at Wake Forest University, nor from the classes in the Oxford Inklings that I have taught at Samford University, at Regent College in Vancouver, and also at my beloved Baylor during the intervening years. These students and many other Tolkienian friends have joined me in forming a latter-day Company of the Little People whose friendship is golden beyond all glitter.

This book is dedicated to my very first student, John D. Sykes Jr. He entered Wake Forest as a freshman from a Baptist parsonage in Norfolk at the same time I entered the university as a teacher fresh from graduate study at the University of Chicago—in 1971. If possible, my gourd was even greener than his. For more than three decades, I have remained a grateful learner from this former student. Like a true hobbit, John has graciously let me receive credit for insights and ideas that truly belong to him. Never was this reversal more fully demonstrated than when Sykes returned to teach in my stead during my National Endowment for the Humanities Fellowship year, 1984–85. There at Wake Forest he began offering a new and instantly popular course called "Faith and Fantasy," which included the entire text of *The Lord of the Rings*. Following his example, I soon began to teach the same course. To my surprise and delight, I came to discern the enduring greatness of Tolkien's book. And in place of a dwindling student audience, I found one that continues to expand even today. Hence my huge double debt to John Sykes—not only for turning my teaching career around, but also for the beginnings of this little book.

Introduction

*T*here is no denying the permanent appeal of J. R. R. Tolkien's epic fantasy-novel, *The Lord of the Rings.* According to three different polls, British readers declared it to be the most important book of the twentieth century. The present study is not devoted to a defense of this extravagant claim. Yet it is most certainly set against the standard explanation of Tolkien's unprecedented readership. Many highbrow critics charge that the masses are drawn to Tolkien because he is an escapist writer. His work, they say, enables its readers to flee from the horrors of modern life, to find refuge in a mythical and unreal world. These critics are right to describe our age as unspeakably terrible. More people were killed by violent means in the twentieth century than in all of the previous centuries combined—roughly 180 million. In our time the ratio of civilian to military deaths has been exactly reversed: from 1:9 to 9:1. Pope John Paul II has rightly called ours "the culture of death."

Yet it is exactly this world of unprecedented evil—of extermination ovens and concentration camps, of terrorist attacks and ethnic cleansings, of epidemic disease and mass starvation and deadly material self-indulgence—that *The Lord of the Rings* addresses. Far from encouraging us to turn away from such evils, Tolkien's book forces us to confront them. Rather than grinding our faces in these horrors, however, it suggests a cure for the ills of our age. This great work enables us to escape *into* reality. Tolkien achieves this remarkable accomplishment by embedding the Gospel as the underlying theme of his book, its deep background and implicit hope.

1

The Lord of the Rings is a massive epic fantasy of more than half a million words. It is also a hugely complex work, having its own complicated chronology, cosmogony, geography, nomenclature, and multiple languages—including two forms of elvish, Quenya and Sindarin. The plot is so grand that it casts backward to the formation of first things, while also glancing forward to the end of time. How could such a huge and learned work—written by an otherwise obscure Oxford philologist—have become an undisputed classic? This book is intended to answer such a question by arguing that much of its staying power resides in its implicit Christianity. The Gospel can be discerned, I will argue, in this book with a pre-Christian setting. But before sketching out the case here to be made, we would do well to attend to three complaints that have repeatedly been raised against *The Lord of the Rings*.

The first is that Tolkien wrote a boy's adventure story that effectively excludes one-half of our race. Tolkien is a male chauvinist, these critics charge, because he includes only a handful of women characters, and because he depicts these few women in highly idealized terms. Quite to the contrary, as we shall discover, Tolkien's women are not plaster figures. Galadriel the elven princess proves to be terrible in her beauty—not treacly sweet and falsely pure; in fact, she is an elf whose importance will diminish once the Ruling Ring is destroyed. So is Éowyn a woman of extraordinary courage and valor, a warrior who can hardly be called a shrinking violet or simpering coquette. Though we see but little of Arwen, the elf-maiden who has surrendered her immortality to wed Aragorn, there is nothing saccharine about her character. Yet even this brief defense of Tolkien's women characters misses the essential point—namely, that Tolkien honors our universal humanity by insisting that the desires of men and women are fundamentally the same, that genital sexuality is not the chief of them, and that we are not divided but united in our basic temptations and sins, our fundamental hopes and longings. Nor is *The Lord of the Rings* a story about boys. Frodo is fifty when he embarks upon the Quest, and Sam is roughly the same age. Only Merry and Pippin can be called youths.

Tolkien is also criticized for creating a rural world that is irrelevant to modern urban life. It is true that the biblical vision of the ideal life is more urban than rural, and that, in the ancient world, existence beyond the city walls was considered barbaric—the realm of robbers and brigands. Yet it is unfair to assume that modern cities have much kinship with the biblical Jerusalem that is exalted as the city of God (Ps. 46:4) and envisioned as the radically renovated city of the world to come (Rev. 3:12). Tolkien regarded our ugly and inhumane cities, far from being the normal state of human existence, as degradations of civilized life.

It should also be remembered that, as the largest city of Europe, London was until recently a patchwork quilt of neighborhoods— each having its own separate identity and distinctive character. Suburban sprawl has not only homogenized the capital city; it has also meant the destruction of the beauty that once characterized rural England. The ruination of the countryside was such a grief to Tolkien that he stopped driving a car once he saw the ruin that highways had caused. Tolkien exalts life in the Shire precisely because it is a domesticated rather than an untamed region. A natural wilderness such as the Forest of Fangorn is an admirable place precisely because it is uninhabited. Yet barbarism results when men and other speaking creatures living in the natural world are not subject to the order of civilization. The city and the wild are meant to be symbiotic, each being humbled and invigorated by the other. And while Tolkien offers the Shire as an exemplary human community, he does not idealize life in Hobbiton. This village is full of the same rivalries and factions and potential evils that plague life in our own towns and cities. Frodo and Bilbo Baggins, for example, have no use for their relatives, the greedy and uppity Sackville-Bagginses.

A third and far more serious complaint against Tolkien's Christian interpreters is that we are wrong to find any traces of the Gospel in his book, since it contains no formal religion. It is true that the hobbits do not pray, although the Númenoreans pause before meals. Neither do the Shire-dwellers build temples or make ritual sacrifices. In extreme distress, however, Sam and Frodo cry out to Elbereth—the elvish name for Varda, who is the wife of Manwë and the compassionate queen of the stars. So is the elven-food called *lembas* clearly reminiscent of the eucharistic wafer: its airy lightness gives strength in direct disproportion to its weight. Yet there is a deeper reason for Tolkien's omission of formal religion from his book. He makes the mythical world of Middle-earth non-religious, among other reasons, in order that we might see Christianity reflected in it more clearly if also indirectly. Readers of *The Silmarillion* are not surprised to learn that a full-fledged theology lies in back of Tolkien's hobbit-books, and that it silently informs *The Lord of the Rings*. As Tolkien himself said, "The religious element is absorbed into the story and the symbolism" (L, 172).

Tolkien's work is all the more deeply Christian for not being overtly Christian. He would have violated the integrity of his art—and thus the faithfulness of his witness—if he had written a 1,200-page novel to illustrate a set of ideas that he could have expressed apart from the story itself. This is a principle not only of good art but also of good theology. God discloses himself in time and space through his people Israel and his son Jesus—not as if they were time-bound manifestations of his timeless nature, but because there is no other way in which God could truly identify himself except through their Story. The religious significance of *The Lord of the Rings* thus arises out of its plot and characters, its images and tone, its landscape and point of view—not from any heavy-handed moralizing or preachifying. Even if we succeed in drawing out a small portion of the novel's huge theological significance, it should send us back to the story itself in eager desire to immerse ourselves again in its rich complexity.

Tolkien clarified this matter considerably in his essay on *Beowulf* entitled "The Monsters and the Critics." There he argued that this seventh-century Anglo-Saxon poem was written by an anonymous Christian, probably a monk, who poetically and faithfully narrated the legend of Beowulf's long battles, first with Grendel, then with his Mother, and finally with the Dragon—a struggle in which, while the monsters are killed, so is Beowulf. The nameless Christian who wrote *Beowulf* sought diligently to preserve the brutality and grimness of the pagan life-world of the ancient Danish legend. Thus does he recount horrible fights and extol fierce loyalties, even as he shows that these ancient warriors were all the more heroic for going down to death without hope of victory: "men with courage as their stay went forward to that battle with the hostile world and the offspring of the dark which ends for all, even the kings and champions, in defeat" (MC, 18).

At the same time, this unnamed Christian poet imbued his non-Christian story with Christian virtues and convictions. "The author of *Beowulf* showed forth the permanent value of that *pietas,*" Tolkien writes, "which treasures the memory of man's struggles in the dark past, man fallen and not yet saved, disgraced but not dethroned" (MC, 23). In *The Lord of the Rings,* Tolkien follows the practice of the *Beowulf*-author. He creates a mythical pre-Christian world where there is not yet a Chosen People, where Abraham and Isaac and Jacob have not yet lived, where Moses has not led Israel out of bondage, where the Hebrew prophets have not spoken the word of the Lord, where God has not become incarnate in Jesus Christ, nor has the church been established nor its Message proclaimed to the nations. Yet for all this, Tolkien's book is pre-Christian only in chronology, not in content. The Gospel resounds in its depths.

This is not to call Tolkien's book a Christian allegory. Tolkien confessed his "cordial dislike" of one-to-one correspondences. To make one thing equal another is for the author to coerce the reader, leaving no room for the free play of the imagination. In the fantasy books of his friend C. S. Lewis, allegory plays a much larger role. If in reading *The Lion, the Witch, and the Wardrobe,* for example, we fail to see that Aslan is a Christ-figure, we have missed the real point of the book. This is nowhere the case in Tolkien. He much prefers fantasy to allegory because it enables "varied applicability to the thought and experience of readers" (1.7). He wants us to discern likenesses and resemblances between the Ruling Ring and the nuclear bomb, for instance, but not to *equate* them. So does Mordor remind us of the death camps and the gulags and the forced re-education farms, but its grimness would be no less deadly to readers who knew nothing of the German and Soviet and Chinese atrocities.

Neither are we meant to identify Gandalf *as* Christ, though he is a wizard who lays down his life for his friends in death and who is then miraculously restored to life. Neither is Frodo the allegorical Son who is sacrificed by Bilbo the Father figure. Tolkien seems to have had a strong sense of the once-and-for-all character of God's revelation in Israel and Jesus. In a real sense, these definitive acts of divine self-disclosure cannot be repeated, not even literarily. Gandalf does not die in atonement for anyone's sins, and if he survives the end of all things it will be because he is one of the maiar, not because, like Christ, he has been resurrected to die no more. Nor does Gandalf alone possess Christ-like qualities. Aragorn and Frodo and Sam Gamgee are also imbued with them. For Tolkien, every Christian is meant to take on the form of Christ. St. Paul admonishes all believers, in fact, to have "the mind of Christ" (Phil. 2:5). Christians are thus summoned to become "little Christs," incarnating our own versions of Gandalf and Aragorn, Frodo and Sam, Faramir and Éowyn.

To speak in this fashion is obviously to go beyond Tolkien's book. We must make clear, therefore, that unlike his friend C. S. Lewis, Tolkien is no sort of evangelist. Tolkien the Catholic is confident that the sacramental and missional life of the church will convey the Gospel to the world without the assistance of his own art. He wants his epic fantasy to stand on its own as a compelling and convincing story, without any adventitious props. Yet it is not apologetics alone that Tolkien seeks to avoid. He is also careful to describe his art as "sub-creation" in order to differentiate it from any sort of illusion—as if it were something entirely invented and thus untrue. Tolkien taught that all human making is a re-forming and re-ordering—for better and worse, for good and ill—of the primary world that God himself creates. Thus does he call his complex fictive world a sub-creation. It is a secondary world of *faërie*—a realm of wonder and enchantment. It has nothing to do with the fairies that Walt Disney reduced to harmless creatures flitting about buttercups. In the elven language called Quenya, *fairë* means spirit, for fairies or elves embody the living spirit of all created things.

The essence of fairy-stories is that they satisfy our heart's deepest desire: to know a world *other* than our own, a world that has not been flattened and shrunk and emptied of mystery. To enter this other world, the fairy tale resorts to fantasy in the literal sense. It deals with *phantasms* or representations of things not generally believed to exist in our primary world: elves (the older word for fairies), hobbits, wizards, dwarves, Ringwraiths, wargs, orcs, and the like. Far from being unreal or fantastic in the popular sense, these creatures embody the invisible qualities of the eternal world—love and death, courage and cowardice, terror and hope—that always impinge on our own visible universe. Fairy-stories "open a door on Other Time," Tolkien writes, "and if we pass through, though only for a moment, we stand outside our own time, outside Time itself, perhaps" (MC, 129). Hence Tolkien's insistence that all fantasy-creations must have the mythic character of the supernatural world as well as the historical consistency of the natural world. The question to be posed for fantasy as also for many of the biblical narratives is not, therefore, "Did these things literally happen?" but "Does their happening reveal the truth?"

We know fantasy to be true when it enables us "to converse with other living things" than ourselves—namely, the animals and plants with which we were once united, but from which we have become alienated in our fallenness (MC, 152). Authentic fantasy enables us to see the creation apart from ourselves and from our degradation of it: to discern that horses may also be dragons, to experience the deeps of the sea as a fish, to visit the heights of the sky as a bird. Such encounters are the chief virtue of fantasy, Tolkien insists, not its vice. He calls fantasy "the most nearly pure form" of art as well as the most potent, at least on the rare occasions when it is achieved (MC, 139). Far from denying and insulting reason, fantasy fulfills its deepest urges. It satisfies even the human appetite for "scientific verity" (MC, 144), Tolkien insists, by overcoming "the drab blur of triteness or familiarity." Only through fantasy are we able to discern the sheer originality and queerness of ordinary things, the surprising strangeness of "stone, and wood, and iron; tree and grass; house and fire; bread and wine" (MC, 146–47).

This final eucharistic phrase points to the heart of the Christian mystery. It is a mystery that, according to Tolkien, lies at the core of fairy-stories. They strike deeper truth than other literary forms precisely because of their happy endings—not in spite of them. True fantasies end happily, thus providing consolation for life's tragedy and sorrow. But their endings are not escapist. Their felicitous outcome is always produced by a dreadful disaster, by a drastic and unexpected turn of events, which issues in surprising deliverance. Tolkien calls this saving mishap a *eucatastrophe*: a happy calamity that does not deny the awful reality of *dyscatastrophe*—of human wreck and ruin. The ending of Tolkien's book is immensely sad because Frodo is too exhausted by his struggle with evil to enjoy the fruits of his victory. Yet the miraculously violent turnabout—the final clash with Sauron that issues in his defeat—reveals that the ultimate truth is joy—"Joy beyond the walls of the world, poignant as grief" (MC, 153).

Tolkien links his word *eucatastrophe* with the word *evangelium*: the one is a good catastrophe and the other is the Good News. Like C. S. Lewis, Tolkien regards many of the world's myths and fairy-stories as forerunners and preparations of the Gospel—as fallible human attempts to tell the Story that only the triune God can tell perfectly. The Gospel is the ultimate fairy-story, Tolkien concludes, because it contains "the greatest and most complete conceivable eucatastrophe. . . . There is no tale ever told that men would rather find was true, and none which so many sceptical men have accepted as true on its own merits. . . . To reject it leads either to sadness or to wrath" (MC, 156).

The Gospel is more than a fairy-story because it is not a human discovery or invention: it is an actuality that occurred in space and time. Christ was actually born, and he actually lived and died and was resurrected. Here is God's own Story wherein the Teller of the tale becomes its chief Actor. Rather than canceling all other stories, however, this one is what they have all been stumbling and pointing toward. The Gospel is the fulfillment and completion of all other stories. Hence the three massive eucatastrophes that Tolkien discerns as forming the essential plot of the Christian story: (1) the Incarnation as the eucatastrophe of human history, as God's taking on human form is met (but not overcome) with the exile of the Holy Family into Egypt as well as the Slaughter of the

Innocents; (2) the Good Friday-and-Easter event as the eucatastrophe of Jesus' own life, as his violent death and vindicating resurrection issue in the world's redemption; (3) the Second Coming as the grand eucatastrophe of both secular and Christian history, when the horrors of Armageddon will produce the unending Joy of life in the world to come:

> [T]his story is supreme; and it is true. Art has been verified. God is the Lord, of angels, and of men—and of elves. Legend and History have met and fused.
>
> But in God's kingdom the presence of the greatest does not depress the small. Redeemed Man is still man. Story, fantasy, still go on, and should go on. The Evangelium has not abrogated legends; it has hallowed them, especially the "happy ending." The Christian has still to work, with mind as well as body, to suffer, hope, and die; but he may now perceive that all his bents and faculties have a purpose, which can be redeemed. (MC, 156)

The Lord of the Rings is the supreme exemplification of this claim made in 1938, sixteen years before Tolkien published his epic fantasy. He would later call his book "a fundamentally religious and Catholic work." Its essential conflict, he insisted, concerns God's "sole right to divine honour" (L, 243). Virtually the entire Gospel can be discerned in this triple-decker that Tolkien labored so diligently, in both mind and body, to bring to completion during the dark years of World War II, often without hope of its ever coming to print. We shall trace the way it discloses—not by overt preachment but by covert suggestion—the principal claims of Christian faith. In so doing, I shall undertake not a scholarly study so much as a theological meditation on *The Lord of the Rings*. Accordingly, I shall use the major doctrines of the Christian faith as the template for my reading of Tolkien.

In chapter one, we shall examine how Tolkien views God's creative activity in the work of Ilúvatar, the All-Father who not only works at the origin of all things but who also remains continually active in the providential order of the world's history. From Creation we shall turn in chapter two to Calamity—to the Fall that occurred even before Middle-earth was made but whose consequences did not infect the whole creation. Our task there will be to fathom the mystery of iniquity—how the rebel Morgoth and his lieutenant Sauron seek both to seduce and overpower the unique children of Ilúvatar: elves and men. We shall be especially concerned to examine more specifically the three deadly powers that the One Ruling Ring affords—invisibility, longevity, and the coercion of will—showing how they remain demonic temptations in our own world no less than in *The Lord of the Rings.*

In the succeeding chapters, we shall seek to plumb the mystery that is far greater and deeper than iniquity—the mystery of goodness and redemption. Because the Gospel is fundamentally good news rather than ill tidings, we will treat Tolkien's positive visions of the Kingdom at considerably greater length. In chapter three, therefore, we will engage Tolkien's profound understanding of the Human Counter-Action that is necessary if the calamity of evil is not to prevail. Here we shall examine the moral and spiritual life as various characters either succeed or fail in cultivating the four cardinal or moral virtues: prudence, justice, courage, and temperance. In chapter four, we will consider the Divine Corrective made possible through the three theological virtues as they are given incarnate life by the hobbits and their friends: faith as friendship, hope as the desire for a fulfillment "beyond the walls of the world," and love as the forgiveness that brings something genuinely new into the world. Finally in chapter five, we shall glance briefly at one of the most puzzling of all paradoxes in Tolkien—why the ending of the Third Age, when wizards and elves were dominant, is not a forecast of catastrophe, and thus why the coming Fourth Age of Men is a sign of Consummation.

Chapter One

The Great Symphony of the Creation

Tolkien's world is thoroughly theocentric. It is inescapably God-centered. The first seventeen pages of *The Silmarillion* contain Tolkien's compelling account of Ilúvatar's creation and sustenance of the universe. Not only is it one of his most original and beautiful pieces of writing, it also serves as the foundation for everything else. The parallels with Genesis are unmistakable. The cosmos as Tolkien envisions it is not a solitary and finished act but an ongoing communal process. Ilúvatar accomplishes his creative will by way of intermediaries that we would call angels but that Tolkien calls valar and maiar. As a universe wherein no one's will is coerced, it contains the possibility of rebellion against Eru, another name for Ilúvatar. Alas, there are valar and maiar who reject his rule. Yet the dissonance that they introduce into Ilúvatar's world cannot silence the harmony that he is determined to bring about. Like the God of the Bible, Ilúvatar refuses to stamp out evil by force. He redeems the world by the uncoercive workings of Providence. It operates not only according to the laws of the natural order, but also with the constant involvement and participation of the divine mind and will. Tolkien describes the providential ordering of the cosmos as "God's management of the Drama" (MR, 329).

The universe as Tolkien conceives it is hierarchical. It is a hugely complex and carefully differentiated universe, forming a great chain of being that stretches from Ilúvatar all the way down to the inert minerals. Yet the hierarchy of Arda (the cosmos) and Eä (the solar system) is not a fixed and frozen order. Tolkien does not give imaginative life to a static universe where (as in much of paganism) everything remains in its original station. On the contrary, there is room for development and alteration. There is also room for choice—and thus for the tragedy and inconsolable grief that are endemic to mortal life. But chiefly it is a universe that features a mighty possibility of growth and change—all prompted by free acts of the will. These actions lead to movement either up or down the great ladder of being. We shall discover wizards and elves, hobbits and men, who are all ascending from lower to higher and *better*, but we shall also encounter those who are descending from higher to lower and *worse*. Just as the most powerful of the valar can commit acts of horrific destruction, so can the lowliest hobbit—like the lowliest and most ordinary person—accomplish deeds of incomparable importance and worth. But they do so only in concord with the essential themes and motifs of Ilúvatar's great symphonic creation.

The Origin and End of Life

Tolkien's pre-Christian world does not know God as Trinity, but rather as the One. Just as the Old Testament is monotheistic, so is there but one God of Middle-earth. Yet in Genesis we hear God somewhat strangely declaring, "Let *us* make man in our image" (1:26). The pronoun may point to the heavenly court, as if God employed intermediate beings to assist him in his action. Christians have rightly seen this plural reference as a foreshadowing of the Trinity, as a sign that God is never alone but that he always exists in triune community.

Tolkien has a similar conception of God as acting communally. Ilúvatar rarely creates in solitude but usually in company. But unlike the Son and Holy Spirit, who are co-creators with the Father, Ilúvatar employs his valar as ancillaries in the act of creation. Nothing even remotely polytheistic is suggested here. The valar are not divinities but subordinate beings whom Ilúvatar has created with the Flame Imperishable of his own Spirit. It is true that, as patrons of the various creative qualities and powers resident in the cosmos, the valar function in ways that are akin to Egyptian or Greco-Roman or Scandinavian deities. Yet nowhere in Middle-earth are they worshiped. On the contrary, the single deity of Arda and Eä is Ilúvatar, who has imbued the entire cosmos with his Spirit. There is nothing, therefore, that does not bear his creative imprint. As Tolkien reiterates endlessly, we ourselves are makers because we have been made. In three immense visions, Eru revealed his cosmic design to the valar and then instructed them to enact it. Tolkien specifies the five stages in Creation as follows:

> a. The creation of the Ainur [valar]. b. The communication by Eru of his Design to the Ainur. c. The Great Music, which was as it were a rehearsal, and remained in the stage of thought or imagination. d. The "Vision" of Eru, which was again only a foreshadowing of possibility, and was incomplete. e. The Achievement, which is still going on. (MR, 336)

The chief task of the valar was to prepare the earth for the coming of the two creatures who are Ilúvatar's own directly created Children—namely, elves and men. Fifteen of these angelic valar are named. They are pure spirits, having no natural bodily existence and thus no mortal limits. Yet they assume shape and gender, both masculine and feminine, in order that the Children of Ilúvatar might know and love them all—except, of course, the one rebel who sought to frustrate Ilúvatar's will for the world.

Tolkien's providentially ordered cosmos is immensely varied and complex. Its unity is not dully monolithic but interestingly differentiated. There are several elven folk, three different groups of men, multiple kinds of dwarves, and scores of fauna and flora with specific and often original names. By giving special qualities and powers to each of these beings, Tolkien reveals the wondrous particularity and divine givenness of many things that we take for granted. Among the valar, for example, Manwë is the noblest and mightiest, and he is known chiefly for his compassion. His spouse Varda made the stars, established the sun and the moon in their courses, and set the morning and evening star Eärendil in the sky. The elves call her Elbereth and Gilthoniel, the Star-Queen and Star-Kindler. Like the Virgin Mary in Catholic and Orthodox tradition, she hears the pleas of both men and elves, coming to their aid. Many religions and philosophies associate light with truth, but Tolkien is distinctively Christian in linking this light with the mercy of Manwë and Varda—just as Jesus the all-compassionate Savior is also called the Light of the World.

The other valar have special powers that serve to enliven our imagination and appreciation of earthly blessings. Aulë is master of crafts and skilled artifacts, and his spouse Yavanna is creator of the Ents, one of Tolkien's most marvelous inventions—the tree-herds. Ulmo ("pourer, rainer") is the lord of waters. Irmo ("master of desire") is the author of dreams and visions, and his spouse Estë ("rest") has created the most beautiful gardens in Valinor, the heaven on earth where the valar dwell. Nienna is the sister of Manwë, and her tears bring healing. Oromë ("horn-blowing") is the great hunter and battler, and his spouse Vána is the special friend of flowers and birds, both of whom rejoice when she is near. Tulkas is the strongest of the valar, loving deeds of prowess and having great gifts of wrestling and running. He is wed to Nessa, who is linked both to deer and dancing, being lithe and swift of foot. These seemingly ordinary gifts are not human accomplishments alone, Tolkien suggests, but also heaven-inspired blessings.

The Omnipresence of Fate, Death, and Doom

It is important to remember that Tolkien is creating a mythical rather than a historical world. Yet Middle-earth has history-like qualities that profoundly link it with our own history and time. Tolkien honors, for example, the deep fatalism that characterizes pagan life—whether it be the contemporary paganism of the late modern West, or the far nobler kind that prevailed in ancient Germany and Scandinavia as well as antique Greece and Rome. For example, Námo, also called Mandos ("prison-fortress"), renders judgment on all those who come to the Houses of the Dead. His spouse Vairë weaves past events into tapestries that tell the history of all things within Time. She perhaps echoes Clotho, one of the three Greek Fates. Clotho spun the web of life, while Lachesis measured its length and Atropos cut it off. Whether in the world of the Greeks or the Norse, Fate is so strong that not even the gods can alter it.

Yet as a Christian writer, Tolkien also modifies the pagan conception of fate to imply its providential direction. Merry and Pippin escape imprisonment at the hands of the orc named Grishnákh when he is killed by a Rider of Rohan just as the orc is about to slay the two hobbits. The narrator makes clear that more than one power is at work here: "An arrow came whistling out of the gloom: it was aimed with skill, or guided by fate, and it pierced [Grishnákh's] right hand." So does the Rohirrim's horse mysteriously avoid trampling the hobbits in the dark: "Whether because of some special keenness of sight, or because of some other sense, the horse lifted and sprang lightly over them; but its rider did not see them, lying covered in their elven-cloaks, too crushed for the moment, and too afraid to move" (2.60).

A pagan sense of Doom—the notion that the world's outcome is unalterably bent toward final destruction—resounds like a dread drumbeat throughout *The Lord of the Rings*. Yet Tolkien also gives the word the triple meaning of destiny, calamity, and judgment. As *destiny*, it signifies that every living thing has its own peculiar mortality; as *calamity* it means that many things end ill; but also as *judgment* it betokens everyone's final state as determined by the just and merciful verdict of Ilúvatar. The double-sidedness of doom is evident in the relation of Mandos and Manwë. As Eru's doom-sayer, Mandos is inflexibly merciless, dealing out judgments where they are justly deserved. Yet Mandos the strict and Manwë the merciful constantly confer with Ilúvatar, who has the ultimate word. Thus does pity balance judgment even in Tolkien's pre-Christian world.

Yet it doesn't banish the lowering cloud that shadows everything. The dour character of heathen life was famously described by the Venerable Bede, an Anglo-Saxon monk-historian of the seventh and eighth centuries. Bede recorded the saying of a Northumbrian chieftain who likened pagan existence to a sparrow flying into one end of a banquet hall and out the other. For the ancients of the far North, everything springs from cold black nothingness, enters into a brief moment of warmth and light called life, and then returns to the dark void whence it came. The monsters that populate the myths of the ancient North are embodiments of this dark void. They are the foes not only of men but also of the gods—both of whom they would finally defeat. In the end, chaos and unreason will triumph. Our Scandinavian and Teutonic forebears were thus mortalists: they believed that Ragnarok would mean the final destruction even of heaven and hell. So are most modern men and women mortalists also—except that the ancient Ragnarok has been replaced with the contemporary dread of terrorist attacks and nuclear strikes. Our only common belief is the fear of death. We fear it because beyond the grave, as the atheist philosopher Bertrand Russell once said, there is nothing. When we die, we rot.

Tolkien refuses to dismiss this dark view of death in either its ancient or modern form. "A Christian," he writes, "was (and is) still like his forefathers a mortal hemmed in a hostile world" (MC, 22). As himself a Christian, Tolkien honors the scandalous hope for the bodily resurrection of the dead that leads to Eternal Life by *not* including it in his pre-Christian epic—lest we think that it is somehow the natural outcome of mortal life. After his battle with the Balrog, Gandalf is not resurrected but resuscitated. He is brought back to life after having been killed. Tolkien knows that, while there have been many resuscitations, there is only one Resurrection. Like Frodo, Gandalf at the end sets sail for the Grey Havens and thence to the unfallen elven realm called Valinor. But this earthly paradise too will one day perish when all things come to their end. Yet beyond or by means of this awful destruction, Arda will ultimately be healed. Tolkien hints at this blessed life to come when, near the end of *The Hobbit*, the dwarf-warrior Thorin Oakenshield bids farewell to Bilbo: "I go now to the halls of waiting to sit beside my fathers, until the world is renewed" (H, 243).

Death is the omnipresent reality in *The Lord of the Rings*. Its presence serves as a caveat against the life-worship that is the unofficial faith of the modern world. The constant iteration of the word "doom" solemnly reminds readers that we are not the final arbiters of our own lives, much less the world's life. Tolkien never lets us forget that no battle is finally won, no victory permanently achieved—not in this world at least—just as every triumph creates a host of new perplexities. The ending of *The Lord of the Rings*—

where the defeat of evil is muted by an enormous grief at the departure of Gandalf and Frodo and Bilbo and the elves—can be read
without tears only by the flint-hearted. C. S. Lewis rightly noted
that a "profound melancholy" pervades the whole of Tolkien's
book, even if the sadness serves to enhance the joy. Haldir the elf
voices this paradox touchingly: "The world is indeed full of peril,
and in it there are many dark places; but still there is much that is
fair, and though in all lands love is now mingled with grief, it
grows perhaps the greater" (1.363).

Lest this poignant realism seem somehow sub-Christian, we
should remember that a melancholy air also infuses much of Scripture, and that Hebrew wisdom is built on an unflinching honesty
about death. It is not surprising to learn that Tolkien helped with
the translation of the Jerusalem Bible, especially the book of
Jonah, the whining prophet, the one who pouts when wicked Nin-
eveh harkens to his prophecy. Yet it is the voices of Job and Isaiah
whose cadences and sentiments resound most clearly in Tolkien's
tragic sense of our human mortality. "Man is born to trouble as the
sparks fly upward" (Job 5:7). "All flesh is grass, and all its beauty
is like the flower of the field. The grass withers, the flower fades,
when the breath of the LORD blows upon it; surely the people is
grass" (Isa. 40:6–7).

More pertinent still for understanding Tolkien's sense of the
world's melancholy is the book of Ecclesiastes. Among its many
memorable lines, perhaps these are the most unforgettable: "The
sun rises and the sun goes down . . . and there is nothing new under
the sun" (1:5, 9). So does the Preacher also declare that "all is van-
ity and a striving after wind" (1:14). Death, in this view, means that
"man goes to his eternal home" (12:5), the tomb. "Remember also
your Creator in the days of your youth, before the evil days come,
. . . before the silver cord is snapped, or the golden bowl is broken"
(12:1, 6). Faramir, the noble warrior of Gondor, echoes such
Hebraic wisdom when he reminds Frodo and Sam that, no matter
how idyllic their life in the Shire may have been, it is like all earthly
beauty and goodness: it cannot last. "Folk must grow weary there,"
Faramir observes of the Shire, "as do all things under the Sun of
this world" (2.290).

It might seem that the elves, because they are immortal, would be sunny and endlessly cheerful creatures. It is not so. Part of their gloom derives from their early rejection of Ilúvatar's will that they live in Valinor. Yet they are somber creatures also because their bodies gradually fade over time. Their long lives enable them to know the entire course of history, from its beginning through its middle and now to the threatened end of Middle-earth. Such comprehensive knowledge of the fallen creation fills the elf Legolas with a deep sadness. "Alas for us all!" he cries. "And for all that walk the world in these after-days. For such is the way of it: to find and lose, as it seems to those whose boat is on the running stream. . . . The passing seasons are but ripples ever repeated in the long long stream. Yet beneath the Sun all things must wear to an end at last" (1.395, 405).

A little-noted change in Tolkien's work occurs between the writing of *The Silmarillion* and *The Lord of the Rings.* In the former, Tolkien is so overwhelmingly indebted to the world of Scandinavian mythology that his outlook remains exceedingly bleak. But when he came to introduce the hobbits into the gigantic mythology he had been creating for many years, Tolkien's vision turned considerably brighter. Perhaps the change is due to the perky character of the hobbits themselves, or perhaps Tolkien came to see how much he remained a Christian even as he was also a lover of things ancient and Anglo-Saxon. In any case, there is an undeniable hopefulness inherent in the hobbit epic. This odd cheer is made evident when Treebeard the Ent reflects on the fundamental transience of earthly existence, now that he has witnessed the orc-slaughter of his precious trees. He finds solace in knowing that, even in defeat, "we may help other peoples before we pass away." Treebeard possesses what might well be called the essential Tolkienian demeanor—a fundamental somberness about the world's state, yet with an overriding joy that cannot be quenched: "Pippin could see a sad look in his eyes, sad but not unhappy" (2.90).

The hobbits and the other Free Peoples always look westward for help, even though it is the place of sunset and thus of the death that brings sadness into the world. Nearly all threat of evil, by contrast, proceeds from the east. Traditional Christian symbolism, by contrast, looks upon the horizon of the rising sun as the locus of hope.

Christians are buried facing eastward, not toward the dying light of the west. Some readers have interpreted Tolkien's exaltation of the west as the sign of a chauvinism that elevates Western Christian culture over the sinister powers of various eastern totalitarianisms—whether Soviet or Chinese or perhaps even German. This ignores the fact that, as a student of ancient languages and peoples, Tolkien knew well that Christianity had already survived the collapse of Greco-Roman civilization, and thus that it can never be equated with the culture of the West. Even if the West were not crumbling, the Gospel would still remain its critic and transformer, never the mere religious expression of occidental cultural life.

The answer to this seeming anomaly lies in Tolkien's confessed desire to write an epic in honor of his own country that, as with ancient epics, would embody the highest virtues and traditions of his people. And since England constitutes the northwest corner of ancient Christendom, and while most of the pagan totalitarianisms of his century came from the east, it is altogether fitting that he should have reversed the traditional geographical symbolism.

Do not laugh! But once upon a time (my crest has long since fallen) I had in mind to make a body of more or less connected legend, ranging from the large and cosmogonic, to the level of romantic fairy-story—the larger founded on the lesser in contact with the earth, the lesser drawing splendour from the vast backcloths–which I could dedicate simply to: to England; to my country. It should possess the tone and quality that I desired, somewhat cool and clear, be redolent of our "air" (the clime and soil of the North West, meaning Britain and the hither parts of Europe; not Italy or the Aegean, still less the East), and, while possessing (if I could achieve it) the fair elusive beauty that some call Celtic (though it is rarely found in genuine ancient Celtic things), it should be "high," purged of the gross, and fit for the more adult mind of a land long now steeped in poetry. I would draw some of the great tales in fullness, and leave many only placed in the scheme, and sketched. The cycles should be linked to a majestic whole, and yet leave scope for other minds and hands, wielding paint and music and drama. Absurd. (L, 144–45)

The Essential Goodness of the Natural Order

The fact that life is shadowed by death does not make it evil. On the contrary, the omnipresence of death renders life immensely precious, even if it can never be the *summum bonum*, our highest good. Tolkien envisions the creation as a blessing and never a curse, just as Yahweh beholds his cosmos and declares it "very good" (Gen. 1:31). Tolkien's world is not the product of a struggle between good and evil deities, as in many pagan religions. Life in Middle-earth is not a contest between equally malign and benign forces—with mortal creatures serving as mere pawns in a great cosmic warfare. Tolkien the Christian refuses any such dualism. On the contrary, all things proceed from Ilúvatar and all things return to him, even though demonic powers come to exercise a frightful force within his world. The elves and dwarves and men and hobbits are wondrously free creatures, not playthings of the gods. Tolkien's cosmos is a vast unitary work whose permanent shape and blessed outcome Ilúvatar has determined from the outset.

Frodo gets a glimpse of the original unmarred goodness of creation when he and the other members of the Company enter the elven realm of Lothlórien created by the elven princess Galadriel. Like the elves themselves, it is a timeless land. Although Galadriel joined her ancestors in rebelling against the will of Ilúvatar, she has preserved Lórien from the shadow of evil. There is an undying quality about Lórien that makes Sam Gamgee feel as if he were "*inside* a song" (1.365). Frodo himself stands awestruck, "lost in wonder," at his first sight of Lórien. It's almost as if he were Adam, the first person to behold the newly minted world, ready to name all the living things, identifying every texture and color and sound:

> It seemed to him that he had stepped through a high window that looked on a vanished world. A light was upon it for which his language had no name. All that he saw was shapely, but the shapes seemed at once clear cut, as if they had been first conceived and drawn at the uncovering of his eyes, and ancient as if they had endured for ever. He saw no colour but those he knew, gold and white and blue and green, but they were fresh and poignant, as if he had at that moment first perceived them

and made for them names new and wonderful. In winter here no heart could mourn for summer or for spring. No blemish of sickness or deformity could be seen in anything that grew upon the earth. On the land of Lórien there was no stain. (1.365)

Ilúvatar's once-unharmed creation has been marred by an evil that corrupts not only the moral life of free creatures; it also lays waste to the natural order. The Dead Marshes are the blasted heath where the corpses of the dead who fell to Sauron and his minions lie visibly preserved beneath the water. This world that was meant to teem with living things has been turned into a forbidding moor. Beyond the marshes lies Mordor itself, Sauron's cruel realm, a vast wilderness of stench and smoke and death:

Here nothing lived, not even the leprous growths that feed on rottenness. The gasping pools were choked with ash and crawling muds, sickly white and grey, as if the mountains had vomited the filth of their entrails upon the lands about. High mounds of crushed and powdered rock, great cones of earth fire-blasted and poison-stained, stood like an obscene graveyard in endless rows, slowly revealed in the reluctant light. . . . The sun was up, walking among clouds and long flags of smoke, but even the sunlight was defiled. (2.239)

As always, Tolkien has our own world in mind when he describes such desolation. He decried the destruction of humane life in our modern cities—not only the poisonous air created by factories and the rabbit-warren crowding of slum housing, but also the repetitive work that dampens the spirit and kills the imagination. He lamented the ravaging of rural England by automobile traffic, and he waxed satirical against those who called him an escapist for creating the fantastic world of Middle-earth: "The notion that motor-cars are more 'alive' than, say, centaurs or dragons is curious; that they are more 'real' than, say, horses is pathetically absurd. How real, how startlingly alive is a factory chimney compared with an elm-tree: poor obsolete thing, insubstantial dream of an escapist!" (MC, 149).

Yet Tolkien the lover of nature is no sentimentalist about it. In one of his last writings, *Smith of Wootton Major*, he declares that the realm of Faërie—the imaginary realm where the ordinary realities of the natural world are made fantastically real—contains marvels that "cannot be approached without danger." Many of its threats, he adds, "cannot be challenged without weapons of power too great for any mortal to wield." Smith's confrontation with the Wind is an example of these perils that belong to the good creation yet remain inimical to human life. Like Job, Tolkien acknowledges the fearful power of earthquakes and tornadoes, of typhoons and disease. They seem to confirm David Hume's contention that "man matters not to nature more than an oyster." In Tolkien no less than Tennyson, nature is "red in tooth and claw," as Smith is made to learn:

> At once the breeze rose to a wild Wind, roaring like a great beast, and it swept [Smith] up and flung him on the shore, and it drove him up the slopes whirling and falling like a dead leaf. He put his arms about the stem of a young birch and clung to it, and the Wind wrestled fiercely with them, trying to tear him away; but the birch was bent down to the ground by the blast and enclosed him in its branches. When at last the Wind passed on he rose and saw that the birch was naked. It was stripped of every leaf, and it wept, and tears fell from its branches like rain. He set his hand upon its white bark, saying, "Blessed be the birch! What can I do to make amends or give thanks?" He felt the answer of the tree pass up from his hand: "Nothing," it said. "Go away! The Wind is hunting you. You do not belong here. Go away and never return!" (SWM, 32)

In penning such a frightening account of nature's antipathy to certain kinds of human life, Tolkien may well have been thinking of Psalm 148:7–8: "Praise the LORD from the earth, you sea monsters and all deeps, fire and hail, snow and frost, stormy wind fulfilling his command!" The trail-blocking snowstorm on Mount Caradhras is another example of inimical natural forces that have no explanation. "There are many evil and unfriendly things in the world," explains Aragorn, "that have little love for those that go on two legs, and yet are not in league with Sauron, but have purposes of their own. Some have been in this world longer than he" (1.302).

The Delights of Bodily Comfort

Not only in Mordor has nature been pillaged and raped. When the Company at last returns to the Shire at the end of their year-long Quest, they discover that an ugly and stench-making industry has been planted in its midst. Their once-organic community has been transformed into a heartless bureaucracy as well. Not the least sign of the joyless new obsession with efficiency and productivity is that all the Hobbiton pubs have been closed. Tolkien is no puritan. As an unabstemious Catholic, he stands in the line of Hilaire Belloc and G. K. Chesterton as a defender of beer and burgundy and all other good things that please the palate and ease the burdens of mortal life. That the hobbits are lovers of ale and pipeweed is a sign not of their self-indulgence but of their *joie de vivre*. They agree with the Psalmist's declaration that "wine . . . gladden[s] the heart of man" (104:15). Beer and tobacco enhance the social life of the hobbits, heightening their enjoyment of each other's company, rather than leading them to solitary addiction. Their delight in these salutary products of Ilúvatar's good creation enables them to raise "the flag of the world," as Chesterton called it.

The drinking song that Frodo remembers at the Prancing Pony in Bree is a joyous salute to "a beer so brown." But it is also a reminder that even a seemingly nonsensical nursery rhyme such as "Hey, diddle, diddle, the cat and the fiddle" probably had its origins in a merry-making occasion. The songs and poems that the hobbits sing and recite serve to deepen our love and sharpen our sense of the delight to be found in ordinary things—and thus of the wonder inherent in such simple gifts as fresh air and broad light, deep sleep and hot baths.

> Sing hey! for the bath at the close of day
> that washes the weary mud away!
> A loon is he that will not sing:
> O! Water Hot is a noble thing!
> . . . .
> is Water Hot that smokes and steams.
> . . . .

and Water Hot poured down the back.
. . . .
O! Water is fair that leaps on high
in a fountain white beneath the sky;
but never did fountain sound so sweet
as splashing Hot Water with my feet!
(1.111)

The hobbits are unabashed lovers of food, enjoying six meals a day. Not for them our late-modern and quasi-gnostic obsession with slimness. Tolkien would have agreed with the novelist Tom Wolfe's lament that America is the country where no one can ever be too rich or too slender. The feast laid on at the Inn of Bree is a celebration of a homely and humble cuisine that features the gift of simple food rather than fastidious gourmandizing: "There was hot soup, cold meats, a blackberry tart, new loaves, slabs of butter, and half a ripe cheese: good plain food, as good as the Shire could show" (1.166). Even Barliman Butterbur's name suggests the hops that he brews and the fat that seasons his cooking. Yet food is far more than physical sustenance for the Company; their shared meals also renew their spirits. Nowhere is their communal existence more fully realized than in their feasting. The sacramental quality of their life is also suggested in the elven waybread called *lembas*. It is light and airy and almost substanceless, giving strength and hope in miraculous disproportion to its heft, feeding the will if not the body.

The hobbits' physique reveals this same paradox that greatness may be found in smallness. Tolkien makes them diminutive creatures in order to challenge our obsession with largeness. For the hobbits, bigger does not mean better, and small can indeed be beautiful. They do not dwell in skyscrapers nor even multistory houses, but in low, tunnelly homes that hug the fertile earth. Their enlarged feet make them swift in movement and adept at tramping the land that they truly *inhabit*. Traveling by foot enables them to appreciate the splendid (and sometimes awful) particularities of the world as faster modes of travel do not.

Tolkien was appalled by our modern obsession with speedy locomotion. It annihilates space, he said, blinding us to the glories that we are traversing. As with much of modern technology, he feared that jet travel is yet another instance of what Thoreau called "improved means to unimproved ends." We take off from New York or Atlanta and land in Cairo or Delhi a few hours later, as if these vastly different cities in vastly different countries were abstract and featureless places, mere dots on a map. No wonder that Tolkien penned a tart note to one year's income tax payment, refusing his support of supersonic jet travel: "Not a penny for Concorde."

As lovers of the good creation, the hobbits are not consumers. They are not convinced that happiness lies in things that can be purchased and devoured; they are not getters and spenders who lay waste to their powers. The hobbits' sod-covered homes, for example, are built to endure and to be permanently occupied, not to be purchased as a speculative investment and then abandoned as soon as the owners can afford something "better." Already in the 1930s, when he was writing both *The Hobbit* and *The Lord of the Rings*, Tolkien discerned that a materialist culture of consumption and convenience was triumphing in the West, and he offered the hobbit way of life as witness against it.

Another sign of the hobbitic love for all humanly created goods is to be found in their refusal to throw things away. They store seemingly useless articles for future use, calling their collected stuff *mathom*. Far from being "junk" that we would discard, these leftovers are precious matter to the hobbits, for the word *mathom* means "treasure" in Anglo-Saxon. So little are hobbits absorbed with their possessions that—like Native Americans at their pot-latch ceremonies—they give rather than receive gifts on their birthdays. Their gift-giving enables them to honor their earthly goods without turning them into idols. Though they know nothing of the Blessed Life to come, they are not far from the Kingdom in heeding the injunction given in the Sermon on the Mount: "Do not lay up for yourselves treasures on earth, where moth and rust consume and where thieves break in and steal" (Matt. 6:19).

It is not surprising to learn that Tolkien thought of himself as a hobbit, and that he identified himself with these creatures whose ambitions and imaginations may be small but whose courage is great. Hence his practice of their humble and self-deprecating habits:

I am in fact a hobbit, in all but size. I like gardens, trees, and unmechanized farmlands; I smoke a pipe, and like good plain food (unrefrigerated), but detest French cooking; I like, and even dare to wear in these dull days, ornamental waistcoats. I am fond of mushrooms (out of a field); have a very simple sense of humour (which even my appreciative critics find tiresome); I go to bed late and get up late (when possible). I do not travel much. (T, 176)

Tolkienian Love of All Things That Grow Slowly, Especially Trees

Most of the free creatures in Tolkien's world reverence the good creation with their craftsmanship. A craft requires lifelong discipline and laborious effort, unlike the instantaneous results of magic. Gandalf's fireworks, by contrast, are matters of skill and labor rather than sorcery—even if his wand seems to be a supernatural gift. Once Gandalf suspects that Bilbo has come into possession of the magical Ruling Ring, he spends many decades in his quest to confirm his hunch. Repeatedly Tolkien stresses the importance of patience, the willingness to avoid the shortcut and the easy way, recommending instead the slow and arduous path that leads to every excellence. Anything worth doing well is worth doing slowly.

The Ents, the fourteen-foot creatures who serve as shepherds of the forest, are telling examples of Tolkien's love of slowness. For them, even the hobbits are too hasty a people. The Ents have taken on the ponderous deliberateness of nature itself, with movements almost as imperceptible as the growth of trees. Hence Pippin's first impression of them:

One felt as if there was an enormous well behind them, filled up with ages of memory and long, slow, steady thinking; but their surface was sparkling with the present: like sun shimmering on the outer leaves of a vast tree, or on the ripples of a very deep lake. I don't know, but it felt as if something that grew in the ground—asleep, you might say, or just feeling itself as something between root-tip and leaf-tip, between deep earth and sky had suddenly waked up, and was considering you with the same slow care that it had given to its own inside affairs for endless years. (2.66–67)

Tolkien has a veritably religious reverence for the natural world. He could name every flower and vegetable that grew in his garden, and he could even distinguish among the kinds of grass. He also had a loving regard for birds, whether the seemingly insignificant sparrows, the messenger-thrush who appears in *The Hobbit*, or the magnificent eagles who deliver Gandalf after his battle with the Balrog, and who also rescue Sam and Frodo at the end of *The Lord of the Rings*. But it was chiefly trees that Tolkien loved. For him, the wanton destruction of forests was akin to the torture and slaughter of animals. He repeatedly vowed to take the part of trees against their enemies: he was an unapologetic defender of nature before environmentalism had yet been made into a cause. Tolkien perhaps speaks for himself when he has Treebeard confess that "nobody cares for the woods as I care for them," and when this same Ent also warns that "the withering of all woods may be drawing near" (2.75–76).

It is not surprising to learn that the forces of evil despise the natural world no less than they scorn the Free Peoples. Ungoliant, the first creature to be corrupted by Melkor, is the enemy of light. Embodied as a hideous spider, she joined Melkor in devouring the Two Trees of Valinor in an obscene vampiric act:

> Then the Unlight of Ungoliant rose up even to the roots of the Trees, and Melkor sprang upon the mound; and with his black spear he smote each Tree to its core, wounded them deep, and their sap poured forth as it were their blood, and was spilled upon the ground. But Ungoliant sucked it up, and going then from Tree to Tree she set her black beak to their wounds, till they were drained; and the poison of Death that was in her went into their tissues and withered them, root, branch, and leaf; and they died. (S, 76)

Tolkien loved trees not only because of their beauty and utility, but also because they share the human rhythm, growing gradually and outliving most other species. In a world maddened by haste and obsessed with speed, Tolkien looked to trees as prime examples of life that has not been made manic with hurry. Already in book 1 we learn the lesson of patience and deliberation when the hobbits take a long time just to arrive at Bree, which is a comparatively short distance from Hobbiton. Their journey to Rivendell takes even longer, as it also proves to be immensely complex and difficult. In all three volumes, the action usually occurs amidst confusion and bewilderment, as the Company often remains uncertain about the events occurring in the larger world that surrounds them. Yet they rarely rush, for to do so is to be made even more confused and bewildered.

Good Magic and Evil Sorcery

Tolkien is thoroughly Christian in not looking to nature for Job's final assurance that the world's harshness does not betoken any divine malignity. Just as Job receives this pledge through the appearance of Yahweh himself, so does Tolkien stress Ilúvatar's own self-identification through the commands he has given to the valar and maiar, and supremely through the redemptive life of the Company itself. Only in the work of those who are good is there providential assurance that the world is morally ordered, and only there lies a way beyond the despair that is likely to be prompted by the hard realities of both the human and natural realms. For Tolkien, malign magic is the product of a panicked despair. It offers a quick and false fix for the complexities and confusions—above all, for the slow and gradual movements—of the good creation.

Magic and divination were common practices in the ancient world, and the Bible displays a good deal of both. King Saul consults the Witch of Endor in order to bring up the spirit of the dead Samuel (1 Samuel 28), even as Simon the Magician wants to learn the secret power inherent in the apostolic laying on of hands (Acts 8). Yet Scripture is clearer still that God's people are meant to eschew magic if it means the manipulation of God's own will and power. Deuteronomy is especially direct:

> When you come into the land which the LORD your God gives you, you shall not learn to follow the abominable practices of those nations. There shall not be found among you any one who burns his son or his daughter as an offering, any one who prac-

tices divination, a soothsayer, or an augur, or a sorcerer, or a charmer, or a medium, or a wizard, or a necromancer. For whoever does these things is an abomination to the LORD; and because of these abominable practices the LORD your God is driving them out before you. (18:9–12)

The New Testament is even stronger in its condemnation of sorcery. It is clearly allied with "the principalities and powers in the heavenly places," with "the world rulers of this present darkness," with "spiritual hosts of wickedness" (Eph. 3:10; 6:12). Far from putting such esoteric forces to divine use, Christians are instructed to wrestle against them. Thus does Paul call the sorcerer Elymas a "son of the devil" and an "enemy of all righteousness." The Apostle blinds Elymas, in fact, for seeking to turn away a Roman proconsul from the Good News (Acts 13:10–11).

Tolkien agreed with C. S. Lewis that modern sorcery gets its real impetus, albeit paradoxically, from modern science. Lewis argues that in the Middle Ages—precisely because they were so thoroughly Christian—very little magic was actually practiced. Serious magical endeavor began, Lewis observes in *The Abolition of Man*, only with the serious scientific projects of the sixteenth and seventeenth centuries. Tolkien notes in a similar vein that, because magic of this sinister kind seeks to alter the primary world, it differs drastically from artistic magic. Gandalf is a wizard whose artistic enchantments heighten our regard for the wonders and mysteries of the natural order. In our own world, by contrast, magic is never an art but always a technique for manipulation: "its desire is *power* in this world, domination of things and wills" (MC, 143). It is also noteworthy that the "hobbits have never, in fact, studied magic of any kind, and their elusiveness is due solely to a professional skill that heredity and practice, and a close friendship with the earth, have rendered inimitable by bigger and clumsier races" (1.10).

Abetted by magic that is bent on power, modern science has come gradually to win our allegiance, whether overtly or covertly. Gradually it has replaced the chief aim of ancient wisdom, both pagan and Christian, which was to conform human life to ultimate reality by way of virtue and knowledge and self-control. As Descartes famously said, the aim of modern science is to render us "masters and possessors of nature." No wonder that Tolkien regarded much of modern technology—precisely because it seeks to put nature under its command, speeding up its deliberate processes—as a disguised form of magic: the attempt to accomplish grand ends by instant means. Machines and magic both serve the cause of what Tolkien called *immediacy*: "speed, reduction of labour, and reduction also to a minimum (or vanishing point) of the gap between the idea or desire and the result or effect" (L, 200). The magic of the machine age is meant for those who are in a hurry, who lack patience, who cannot wait. He thoroughly agreed with Winston Churchill's claim, made in the midst of World War II, that ours is "a dark age, [made] more sinister and perhaps more protracted by the lights of perverted science." Churchill also described the then-new devices of radar and similar methods of electronic spying as "wizard war."

Treebeard the Ent reports that Saruman, once he becomes obsessed with power, acquires "a mind of metal and wheels; and he does not care for growing things, except as far as they serve him for the moment" (2.76). Saruman has made his fortress at Isengard into a prison house of mechanical power. Like Sauron, he has created weapons of horror, thus perverting the good skills he learned from Aulë. Isengard thus resembles sights that Tolkien surely saw in his boyhood Birmingham. It is

> a graveyard of unquiet dead. For the ground trembled. The shafts ran down by many slopes and spiral stairs to caverns far under; there Saruman had treasuries, store-houses, armouries, smithies, and great furnaces. Iron wheels revolved there endlessly, and hammers thudded. At night plumes of vapour steamed from the vents, lit from beneath with red light, or blue, or venomous green. (2.160)

Sauron is a sorcerer precisely in this mechanical fashion: he uses his craftsmanship for the sake of power over others. He fashions the One Ring in order to put the other rings under his domination. As a practitioner of the black arts, he is rightly called Necromancer (1.263), just as Angmar, king of the Ringwraiths, is rightly called Sorcerer: "because of his cunning he grew ever higher in the Lord's

[Sauron's] favour; and he learned great sorcery, and knew much of the mind of Sauron; and he was more cruel than any orc" (3.164).

While Tolkien linked modern machines to both ancient and modern magic, it is important to discredit the common view that Tolkien was a Luddite who damned and dismissed modern technology as evil and godless. There is little doubt that he regarded pre-modern existence as in many ways superior to our own, and that he lamented our enslavement to highly specialized means of manufacture, since many of them are designed to hurry and even to crunch time. But Tolkien was also careful to point out that the use of a thing—whether for good or ill—determines its worth, not the thing itself. The ancient adage—*abusus non tollit usus* (the abuse of a thing does not take away its proper use)—is at least as old as St. Augustine. To deny its truth is to indulge in an anti-modern misanthropy that denies the inventive spirit implanted by God in all free creatures—as if the Holy Spirit were absent from modernity.

Tolkien approvingly cites the Noldor elves as having the spirit of modern "'science and technology,' as we should call it." Their interest in ingenious craftsmanship, he adds, is akin to that of Christians engaged in scientific research resulting unhappily in malign byproducts. Tolkien cites poisonous gases and explosives as examples. Such scientists are not dealing with "necessarily evil" things, Tolkien insists. Yet the sinister "nature and motives of the economic masters who provide all the means" for such research dictate that its products will almost certainly be put to evil purposes (L, 190). For Tolkien, the means are altogether as important as the ends. Scientific experiments and technological achievements must be good in themselves, he insisted, and not good merely in the ends they serve. Medicines that stop ravaging diseases could not be justified, for example, unless they are produced by humane methods.

The Supreme Gift of Speech

Tolkien takes the Creation accounts in Genesis and the Prologue to the Fourth Gospel with utmost seriousness. Genesis records God as *speaking* the cosmos into being, and the fourth evangelist declares

God to be the Logos who stands at the beginning of things, even as he declares Jesus Christ to be the Logos who has become flesh. Christians are by definition Logocentrists: we believe that the incarnate Logos is the center of the cosmos. Because God himself is understood fundamentally as the Word, Tolkien regards speech as our most fundamental gift, the one thing that distinguishes us as uniquely human creatures made in the image of God. When human breath becomes articulate—when our species stops grunting and starts speaking—we become drastically distinct from other beings. The glory of plants and animals and mountains is to be simply and inarticulately what they are. Human uniqueness derives, by contrast, from what we make—from our capacity to subcreate, to rearrange the good things of the good creation so as to make them even better—or, alas, much worse. And speech is the chief means for all human creativity and destructivity.

Through language, Tolkien argues, we become capable of purposes and designs, of objects and intentions, that are good not only for ourselves but also for others—and ultimately for God. Indeed, speech was the gift of Eru to elves and men and Ents. All of us speaking creatures can use our word-and-thing-making faculties for evil as well as good. But we would be neither speakers nor hearers nor makers at all were we not products of the Creator. From the smallest act of choosing our clothes to the grandest scientific hypothesis or the most splendid symphony or fresco, we make because we have been made, as Tolkien declares in "Mythopoeia":

> Man, Sub-creator, the refracted Light
> through whom is splintered from a single White
> to many hues, and endlessly combined
> in living shapes that move from mind to mind.
> Though all the crannies of the world we filled
> with Elves and Goblins, though we dared to build
> Gods and their houses out of dark and light,
> and sowed the seeds of dragons—'twas our right
> (used or misused). That right has not decayed:
> we make still by the law in which we're made.
>
> (MC, 144)

Though words are never adequate to the things they specify, neither are they mere arbitrary vocables invented for our selfish manipulation of people and things. Tolkien the Christian holds that our *logoi* (words) are rooted in the *Logos* (the Word). Mythologies are supreme examples of the ontological character of speech: words are grounded in the world's own being. They disclose—through characters and events and images—the fundamental order of things, an order that we do not invent so much as discover. As Tolkien says in his essay "On Faërie Stories," "The incarnate mind, the tongue, and the tale are in our world coeval" (MC, 122). They emerge simultaneously, so that man the speaker is already man the storyteller.

Tolkien believed that he had not *devised* his magnificent mythical world so much as he had *found* it—indeed, that it had been revealed to him by God. Once when asked what a certain passage in *The Lord of the Rings* meant, he replied: "I don't know; I'll try to find out." "Always I had the sense," he declared, "of recording what was already 'there,' somewhere: not of 'inventing'" (T, 92). The tales arose in his mind, he confessed, "as 'given' things, and as they came, separately, so too the links grew" (T, 92). Tolkien thus came to regard his characters and their realm not as fictional but as historical persons and places! Venice, he confessed, was like "a dream of Old Gondor."

Tolkien's unparalleled mastery of ancient tongues convinced him that words are rooted in reality because speech arises out of experience. As C. S. Lewis observed of Tolkien, "He had been inside language" (T, 134). Against the reductionist view that "language is a disease of mythology," therefore, Tolkien argued that in myth lies the real origin and continuing power of language. The name for the Norse thunder-god Thor (from which we get our "Thursday") probably came into being, for example, as some ancient Norseman experienced three things at once: human rage in the form of a bellowing, hot-tempered, ox-stout farmer; the raucous noise of lightning and thunder; and the divine power to which human life is always subject. Owen Barfield, the one real philosopher among the Oxford Inklings, made a similar point about the Latin *spiritus* and the Greek *pneuma* and the Hebrew *ruach*.

Unlike our one-dimensional word *spirit*, these three antique words mean wind-breath-spirit simultaneously. For ancient Greeks and Romans and Israelites to have uttered such words was for them to have experienced—without any disjunction—the tremendous power of natural force, the invisible sign of human life, as well the nearness and might of divine reality.

The original metaphoric and mythological richness of ancient languages, Tolkien argued, has been largely lost in modern tongues, so that our own language is far thinner than that of our forebears. He disdained the popular notion that poetry and myth are primitive means of communication that need to be replaced by the more precise abstractions of modern science. The myth of Thor, according to this mistaken view, is a crude prescientific attempt to explain the phenomenon that we know to be the result of hot and cold air clashing. For Tolkien, this is to get things exactly backward. The truth is that modern languages have degenerated rather than improved. In the ancient world, men and women did not abstract ideas and concepts from their complex rootage in the interwoven (though unequal) dimensions of existence: the natural, the human, the divine and, alas, the demonic.

It is precisely when words are uprooted from their concrete origins and converted into empty abstractions that they can be put to wicked purposes. We need not look only to modern political rhetoric as proof of this danger; Saruman illustrates it all too well. Partly because he knows that he has Gandalf's respect, Saruman urges his fellow wizard to join with him in an alliance with Sauron. Together they would use the power of the Ring to accomplish good rather than ill. Saruman argues for the use of evil means to accomplish noble ends by appealing eloquently to high ideals.

> We can bide our time, we can keep our thoughts in our hearts, deploring maybe evils done by the way, but approving the high and ultimate purpose: Knowledge, Rule, Order; all the things that we have so far striven in vain to accomplish, hindered rather than helped by our weak or idle friends [i.e., hobbits and men]. There need not be, there would not be, any real change in our designs, only in our means. (1.272–73)

Saruman's moral duplicity is not the only evil here condemned. Tolkien also reveals that brilliant rhetoric can disguise foul purposes. When Saruman speaks from his tower called Orthanc ("Cunning Mind"), he addresses the Company with a voice that is "low and melodious, its very sound an enchantment. . . . [A]ll that it said seemed wise and reasonable, and desire woke in them by swift agreement to seem wise themselves. When others spoke they seemed harsh and uncouth by contrast" (2.183). Saruman employs slick words to prettify his ugly argument. But just as Gandalf had earlier broken the enchantment of Saruman's speech by discerning its cruel logic, so does Gimli detect what is false in this later example of Saruman's honeyed language. Though dwarves can often seem obtuse, this one acts like an early George Orwell writing *Animal Farm*. Gimli penetrates Saruman's perverse attempt to overturn the meaning of ordinary terms by giving them pleasing expression: "The words of this wizard stand on their heads. . . . In the language of Orthanc help means ruin, and saving means slaying, that is plain" (2.184).

In order to guard against the use of high-sounding abstractions for wicked ends, Tolkien employs harsh sounds to convey the harsh character of evil. In *The Hobbit*, he refers to the demons who seek to destroy Bilbo and the dwarves as "goblins." Yet this word has come to connote mere mischievousness, as in Emerson's saying that "A foolish consistency is the hobgoblin of small minds." Thus does Tolkien call them orcs in *The Lord of the Rings*. The hard sound of this Anglo-Saxon word for "demons" clearly conveys the evil character of these man-eating monsters. Melkor first bred them from elves whom he had captured and tortured, having then twisted and mutilated them into cruel parodies of themselves.

Tolkien also enriches our regard for words whose original metaphoric meaning we have now lost. For example, Frodo's sword is called Sting, not because it gives the small hurt of a needle's prick or an insect's bite, but because it has the power to *pierce* enemies—as in its original Anglo-Saxon meaning. Tolkien readers pondering St. Paul's plangent cry "O death, where is thy sting?" (1 Cor. 15:55) will now know that the Apostle is not hailing the risen Christ's victory over a mere pinching injury, but the deathly agony of a sword-thrust. So does Tolkien's word *shirriff* remind us that our *sheriff* comes from *shire*, which in turn means county or region. A sheriff is thus a person who helps keep order in a specified district. In the peaceful world of the Shire, the shirriffs merely patrol the borders and capture stray animals. Even so, their name reveals how rich mythological and linguistic allusions underlie almost all of Tolkien's borrowed words. Most of them are drawn from Norse and Teutonic and Celtic myths, but *sauros* is the Greek word for "lizard." The Satanic figure called Sauron is thus linked to a cold-blooded reptilian, as in the Garden of Eden.

Tolkien is no mere antiquarian in his love of ancient words. He is also the inventor of new and morally resonant names. The Ringwraiths, for instance, are so called because they are men who have yielded to Sauron for so long they have become entirely disembodied creatures who nevertheless wear cloaks, ride horses, and wield weapons. But their real terror lies in their malice, their Sauronic cruelty and spite. As Tom Shippey has shown, their name is linked to the Anglo-Saxon *writhan*, which serves as the root of our modern words *wraith* and *wreath*. The Ringwraiths are as ghostly as rising smoke, but they are also creatures twisted with anger. For our word *wrath* also derives from *writhan*. Thus does Tolkien teach an important moral lesson through the etymological richness of *Ringwraith*: the deadly sin of wrath knots us in a rage that withers our real substance. The larger point to be taken is that, for Tolkien, language is never neutral. As our most precious gift, it is always loaded with implication, always employed for either good or ill.

It is especially noteworthy that various members of the Company, especially the hobbits, repeatedly have recourse to poetry and song. Speech at its fullest stretch is found in rhyme and meter, in alliteration and assonance and consonance, as well as in many other poetic devices. When sung, poetry takes on even greater import, as it lifts words into the higher dimension of shared celebration or else plunges them into the depths of communal lament. This is not to say that poetry is an unalloyed good. Sauron's poem, like the incantation of the Barrow-wights, is an enchantment in the literal sense: its drumbeat cadences and repetitions cast a sinister spell over its hearers:

Ash nazg durbatulûk, ash nazg gimbatul, ash nazg
thrakatulûk agh burzum-ishi krimpatul.
One Ring to rule them all, One Ring to find them,
One Ring to bring them all, and in the Darkness bind them.

(1.267)

Most often the hobbits sing for joy rather than consolation, for in their singing they break into a transcendent realm beyond their own small world. Aragorn's songs also tell of elves, and thus serve to give the Quest its proper setting. Nearly all of the songs in *The Lord of the Rings* remind readers and characters alike that, evil though Sauron surely is, and grave though the struggle against his forces will surely remain, the Quest belongs to a much larger and older drama than their own immediate failure or success might indicate.

That the words of Tolkien's poems and songs are simple and the rhymes predictable counts nothing against them, for they are not intended as timeless art but as bracing verse. The modern disdain for conventional poetic forms has been bought at a terrible price, in Tolkien's estimate. It means that most people no longer have poems rattling around in their heads, either to cheer or to comfort. Ours is a prosaic world in more ways than one. The hobbits' best songs, by contrast, enable them to embrace both bright freedom and dark fate, as in Merry and Pippin's modification of the dwarf song that had set Bilbo on his original adventure:

Farewell we call to hearth and hall!
Though wind may blow and rain may fall,
We must away ere break of day
Far over wood and mountain tall.

To Rivendell, where Elves yet dwell
In glades beneath the misty fell,
Through moor and waste we ride in haste,
And whither then we cannot tell.

With foes ahead, behind us dread,
Beneath the sky shall be our bed,
Until at last our toil be passed,
Our journey done, our errand sped.

We must away! We must away!
We ride before the break of day!

(1.116)

The Redeeming Hierarchy of Ilúvatar's Universe

Tolkien envisions Ilúvatar as making the universe into a vast song, a powerful symphony, "a Great Music." Like all complex creations, Tolkien's fantasy world is a realm in which each part must be subordinated to the whole, the lesser to the greater. The idea of hierarchy is much out of fashion in our egalitarian time because there seems to be something inherently unjust about declaring certain things to be better than others by their very nature. Yet Tolkien believes that our loss of hierarchy signals a larger moral and religious loss as well: we are deprived of the means for rightly ordering our lives. Together with St. Augustine and the whole Christian tradition, Tolkien holds that the essential task of all people is to set their loves in order: to love the triune God first and last, and to love all other things in right relation to him. Tolkien provides a hierarchically structured world so as to aid us in this task. Each order of being has its own unique use and indispensable place, so that nothing is degraded in belonging to a lower rather than a higher order. On the contrary, everything is thereby exalted in serving precisely the purpose for which it was made. In no way is anyone or anything debased by the fact that others serve higher functions, nor is there any condescension toward others who have lesser tasks.

The lowest of things are the inert minerals of the earth, and yet even they contain precious stones that can be hewn and polished into things of great beauty—just as they can also become objects of an enslaving lust. Above them are the various plants, many of them essential to healing. Trees, as we have seen, are the most magnificent botanical species, and their caretakers the Ents are among Tolkien's most original creations. Higher still are the many kinds of animals, not only because they are mobile but also because many of them possess the consciousness that makes them real companions. Horses are perhaps the most splendid of Tolkien's animate creatures, and they remain central to Tolkien's world—whether in Gandalf's swift Shadowfax or Sam's humble pony Bill.

The dwarves are among the least savory of the Free Peoples, perhaps because they were created by the vala Aulë in his desire to hasten the work of Ilúvatar. Aulë impatiently wanted to behold the men and elves whom Ilúvatar himself would create. Perhaps because their original existence was not willed by Ilúvatar, the dwarves remain rather possessive, isolated, non-cooperative, and wrathful creatures dedicated to delving the earth. Yet because Aulë created them in affirmation rather than rejection of Ilúvatar's own creativity, Ilúvatar later confirmed the worth of dwarves. Repeatedly in *The Lord of the Rings*, we encounter those who have sinned by excessive zeal—rather than in overt rejection of the good. The products of such zealous sin are almost always forgiven and turned to good purposes. The dwarves, for example, excel as miners and workers of metal and stone. Their fierce indomitability in battle also frees them from subjection to Sauron. They are also to be honored for having created magnificent underground civilizations.

At the center of Tolkien's hierarchy stand the two fully human creatures: men and hobbits. While the hobbits are small-statured, they clearly belong to our own species. As the younger children of Ilúvatar, men are not only morally but also physically and culturally diverse. In *The Lord of the Rings*, we encounter three groups among the Men of Gondor: the Dúnedain or Men of the West, the Men of the Twilight such as the Rohirrim, and the Men of Darkness or Wild Men who have a lesser stature and nature. Both hobbits and men are subject to aging and illness, they are ignorant of the future, and they are not always able to comprehend the minds of other races. Yet the Third Age marks the beginning of their rise to dominance and, because of their capacity for free obedience to Ilúvatar, they may come to dwell with him in the End. As we shall discover, the Age of Men shall excel even that of elves and wizards, because in one of them Ilúvatar shall assume human form.

Frodo and Sam's moral development reveals that each order of being provides extraordinary room for either growth or deterioration. Though he is the noblest of hobbits, Frodo becomes far better than he was at the beginning of the Quest. The bumbling peasant Sam rises, in turn, from the virtual bottom of the social hierarchy to become the hero of the entire book and the eventual mayor of Hobbiton. Gollum demonstrates, alas, how hobbit life can be grotesquely degraded by evil. So is Aragorn the best of men, though he too experiences considerable moral growth. On the other hand, the Ringwraiths—once bearers of the nine rings made for men—have degenerated into horrible parodies of humanity. In no case are any creatures petrified within their original condition, for they have all either ascended or descended according to their good or evil use of freedom, and in right or wrong relation to Ilúvatar's redeeming purpose.

Above men stand the elves, the firstborn children of Ilúvatar. They seem to represent the eternal and supernatural element in human life. As we have noticed, they do not naturally die, though they can be slain, even as they can die of grief. They are the fairest of Ilúvatar's creatures and the most akin to him in spirit. As lovers of all natural things, especially stars and waters, they have had a tense relation with the earth-delving dwarves. Tall and slender, the elves have a keen sense of hearing and sight, and they have a remarkable talent for communication. In fact, they have given language to the other speaking species. Elves are so resilient that they need little or no sleep, but rest their minds by beholding beautiful things, especially the stars. The elves are by nature good, though they can be seduced by evil. They can also marry outside their race—as with Luthien and Beren, Arwen and Aragorn. Luthien and Arwen surrender their immortality in order that they may be united in death with their mortal spouses.

Tolkien gave an exceedingly unfortunate name to the new mortality taken on by these self-sacrificing elves: he called it reincarnation (L, 189). Yet the elven-maiden Arwen is not reincarnated in Hindu fashion. She does not begin a completely new life, one utterly unlike her former existence, because of any meritorious or reprehensible acts she has done in some previous life. Instead, Tolkien offers a powerful imaginative analogy between the immortal Arwen's decision to become a mortal woman and the Son of God's refusal to regard his equality with the Father as a thing to be grasped. Just as Christ empties himself of his divine eternality in order to assume the form of a mortal servant and to become obedient unto death, even crucifixion, so *in her infinitely smaller way* does Arwen give up her undying life to perish alongside her beloved Aragorn. Elves who so surrender their immortality in order to be joined in death with their beloved serve as a distant echo of Christ's own incarnation as it is described in the early Christian hymn recorded in Philippians 2. Yet these mortality-assuming elves are utterly unlike Christ because they do not die in atonement for anyone's sins. Nor are they resurrected. In the end, most of the faithful elves will be joined with the valar in Valinor.

Higher still than the elves are the maiar. Like all other beings made by Ilúvatar, they are not creatures of a fixed fate. Gandalf and Saruman, as well as Sauron and the Balrog, are maiar who demonstrate this principle. While the Balrog and Sauron have sunk to sheer evil, Saruman and Gandalf move in opposite directions on the scale of goodness. Saruman the White begins as a righteous wizard for whom Gandalf has the utmost regard. Yet Saruman is gradually corrupted by his Faustian desire for unbridled knowledge, especially Ring lore that would teach him the ways of Sauron. From having been a high wizard, therefore, he ends as a disgusting sorcerer, and in so doing he loses all distinctness of color. Evil literally defaces those who practice it.

Saruman's final insignificance is demonstrated by his murder at the hands of his despicable lieutenant Wormtongue, who was originally a splendid human corrupted by Saruman. Gandalf the Grey, by contrast, is so ennobled by his many counsels of wisdom and his many deeds of courage that he emerges as Gandalf the White, virtually beatified. Above the maiar are ranked the valar, and they too have the potential to act either in accord with Ilúvatar's will or else against it. Manwë and his spouse Varda are filled with such compassion and mercy that they have become the dearest of valar to Ilúvatar, while Melkor in his rejection of the divine music has sunk into the clanging abyss of evil. At the top of the hierarchy, Ilúvatar himself reigns—not in omnipotent domination of the cosmos, but in majestic honor and splendor and love for all that he has made.

The single figure who seems not to fit within Tolkien's cosmic scheme is Tom Bombadil. On the one hand, he and his spouse Goldberry resemble a wood-sprite (or dryad) and a water-nymph—so fully do they belong to the natural world. Yet Bombadil calls himself the Eldest, saying that he was present before the rivers and the trees. As a figure who is somehow prior to nature, he will outlast all other things, until in the End he too perishes. On the other hand, Tom and Goldberry bear a certain likeness to the unfallen Adam and Eve, so innocent are they of all moral complexity. They seem not so much to have resisted temptation as to be immune from it. The Ring, for instance, has no effect on Bombadil. He does not disappear when wearing it, and he can still see Frodo when the hobbit has it on his finger. And while Bombadil rescues the hobbits from Old Man Willow, he acts not from a sense of friendship or justice, so much as in desire to protect his territory.

Bombadil seems oblivious to all moral distinctions. He seems to dwell joyfully in the world without any possibility of defecting from his service to Ilúvatar. Perhaps Tolkien wants his readers to discern the presence of other such creatures who dwell delightfully beyond good and evil. But while being an immensely interesting figure who rescues the hobbits from the Barrow-wights as well as Old Man Willow, Bombadil is morally and spiritually irrelevant to the struggle that lies at the heart of the Quest. As Gandalf wisely observes, Bombadil would be an utterly unfit keeper of the Ring: he would either forget it or even throw it away. "Such things have no hold on his mind" (1.279). Perhaps he is Tolkien's reminder that, while the world's hierarchy is carefully calibrated for our benefit, it contains anomalies that lie beyond our comprehension. Like the emblem placed atop the tallest spire when a medieval cathedral was finally finished, Bombadil may be Tolkien's own monkish gift to Ilúvatar—a creature not meant for our understanding but for the enjoyment of God alone.

The Moral Challenge of Middle-earth History

The presence of an amoral and ahistorical creature such as Bombadil reveals, by his very exceptionality, that Tolkien's world is intrinsically moral and historical. Though it is a magical realm that Tolkien entirely invented, it is not a mythic "once upon a time" story. Myths of this sort occur in a timeless realm in order to illustrate timeless truths. They can often be summarized in abstract statements: "Appearances can be deceiving"; "Beware of strangers offering gifts"; and so on. The order of such myths is usually circular, repetitive, and unchanging; reincarnation is often one of their features. They have no necessary link with any particular events or peoples, and in them the future is essentially identical to the past. Everything goes around in a gigantic circle of virtual sameness.

Tolkien's mythical world, by contrast, is thoroughly historical. No event is ever repeated, and every creature has unique importance. One era is always the moral consequence of another. In fact, the historical continuity of Tolkien's successive ages resembles the story of Israel and Christ and the church. Just as lowly Israel eventually became a mighty kingdom, so did the First and Second Ages reveal the grand accomplishments of wizards and elves and dwarves. The Third Age seems to entail a considerable decline. It is an epoch rather like the waning Israelite world into which Jesus was born, where the temple in Jerusalem would soon be destroyed. Yet Christ's life and death and resurrection brought about a revolutionary rekindling of hope, not only for Israel but for the Gentile world as well. So does the Third Age mark the surprising union of greater and lesser creatures—elves and dwarves—with hobbits and men in order to accomplish the seemingly impossible: the defeat of Sauron. The dawning of the Fourth Age of Men would not seem to be bright with promise, but neither did the early years of the church augur the spread of the Gospel to the whole world. In many other ways does Middle-earth resemble human history, and therein lies its credibility. "History often resembles 'Myth'," Tolkien declares, "because they are both ultimately of the same stuff" (MC, 127).

It is often noted that our modern sense of history—whereby we read events as the result of complex moral actions rather than arbitrary cosmic forces—has been given to us by the historical faith of Judaism and Christianity. To suggest the pertinence of this legacy for his own mythical world, Tolkien makes the geography of

Middle-earth resemble northern Europe, with the Shire being some-what analogous to England. It is a historical realm because, at least within its mortal limits, its future is completely unknown. It depends on the engagement of all the Free Peoples against Sauron and his evil forces, but it also depends on the silent and providential workings of the will of Ilúvatar within the events of Middle-earth.

Repeatedly we are reminded that Bilbo did not merely find the Ring, but that in a mysterious sense the Ring found him. For while the Ring is being manipulated by Sauron, who is determined to regain control of it, it is also subject to Ilúvatar's far greater power. "Behind [the Ring's abandonment of Gollum] there was some-thing else at work," Gandalf explains to Frodo, "beyond any design of the Ring-maker. I can put it no plainer than by saying that Bilbo was *meant* to find the Ring, and *not* by its maker. In which case you also were *meant* to have it" (1.65). Because divine will is slow-working, uncoercive, and mysterious, Frodo and the Company know little more than that Ilúvatar's final victory will occur in the Last Eucatastrophe. There the Dagor Dagorath—Middle-earth's equivalent of the biblical Armageddon—will bring the grand sym-phony of creation into a violent but final harmony through the heal-ing and remaking of Arda. In the meantime, all the inhabitants of Arda dwell amid drastic uncertainty. Thus does Gandalf declare at the Council of Elrond that the Company must undertake the Quest for the sake of a good far greater than the benefit of their own pass-ing age: "We should seek a final end of this menace, even if we do not hope to make one" (1.280).

Humanity's wondrous and terrible ignorance of the future gives time its enduring ethical and religious importance. It means that we are at once radically dependent upon everything that has come before us, but also that we are radically responsible for everything that comes after us. Sam Gamgee gradually discovers this deep moral truth. Slowly he comes to discern that the long-lasting tales deal with people who did not seek to find a more interesting life or to make a place for themselves in history. The real heroes are peo-ple who "just landed" in the tales that are told about them—ordi-nary people who found themselves unexpectedly called upon to act courageously and selflessly.

The Call to the Life of the Quest

Their stories are later remembered, Sam observes, because these folks—usually against their own wishes—were embarked upon a Quest, a mission whose outcome involved something immensely larger and more important than their own happiness. In explaining this matter to Frodo, Gandalf draws a fundamental distinction between a quest and an adventure. An *adventure*, he says, is a "there-and-back-again" affair. One undertakes an adventure as a matter of one's own desire—often from boredom and a lust for excitement. Once the treasure is found and the adventure is over, one returns essentially unchanged by the experience. An escapist culture lives for adventures. A *Quest*, by contrast, is never a matter of one's own desire but rather of one's calling. Over and again, Frodo asks why he has been chosen for his dreadful task. His summons is not to find a treasure but to lose one—to bear the Ring back to the Cracks of Doom and there to cast it into the melting fires whence Sauron first forged it.

Frodo and his friends have no guarantee, not even the likelihood, that their Quest will succeed. They will be moving ever more certainly toward danger, never away from it toward any kind of permanent safety. Bilbo has composed a walking song that gives them courage and determination. Frodo's early quotation of his mentor's song reveals the younger hobbit's burgeoning wisdom:

> *The Road goes ever on and on*
> *Down from the door where it began.*
> *Now far ahead the Road has gone,*
> *And I must follow, if I can,*
> *Pursuing it with weary feet,*
> *Until it joins some larger way,*
> *Where many paths and errands meet.*
> *And whither then? I cannot say.*
>   (1.82–83)

In an earlier version of his song, Bilbo had used the word "eager" rather than "weary," but age and experience have shown him that life drains even as it fulfills. Yet Bilbo's exhaustion in no way diminishes his conviction that everyone has an "errand"—a mission and purpose—and that everyone undertakes a journey every day of one's life. We are all bound on the same Road toward death—indeed, beyond death. We are immersed in the river of time—the "ever-rolling stream" which, in Isaac Watts's splendid rendering of the Ninetieth Psalm, "bears all its sons away." To deny the constant nearness of death is, for Tolkien, the supreme folly. About the basic transience of life, as in so much else, he is in thorough accord with Scripture: "Come now, you who say, 'Today or tomorrow we will go into such and such a town and spend a year there and trade and get gain'; whereas you do not know about tomorrow. What is your life? For you are a mist that appears for a little time and then vanishes. Instead you ought to say, 'If the Lord wills, we shall live and do this or that'" (Jas. 4:13–15).

The Company's quest to destroy the Ring—having no guarantee of success but rather the immense likelihood of failure—is not unlike the journey of life. The path is full of such perils that our destiny can never be predicted in advance. Legolas the elf declares this dark truth: "Few can foresee whither their road will lead them, till they come to its end" (2.95). The question—and thus the Quest—concerns how we shall travel the road and whether we shall complete our errand. Like Frodo, we are called not so much to find a treasure as to lose one. There is a huge difference, of course. While the Ring is evil and must be destroyed, our lives are good and must be preserved. Yet they are not to be preserved at all costs. Rather we are called eventually to surrender the bounty given to us at our birth. The struggle for the good against the evil requires nothing less than everything—the giving up of our lives—whether sooner or later, whether bitterly or graciously, whether by happenstance or intention.

Tolkien's work is imbued with a mystical sense of life as a journey or quest that carries us beyond the walls of the world. To get out of bed, to answer the phone, to respond to a knock at the door, to open a letter—such everyday deeds are freighted, willy-nilly, with eternal consequence. From the greatest to the smallest acts of either courage or cowardice, we travel irresistibly on the path toward ultimate joy or final ruin. According to Bilbo, we can "keep our feet"—i.e., we can avoid being swept away to the permanent death that comes from having failed our mission—only so long as we have a sure sense of where we are supposed to be going and how we may rightly arrive there.

> [Bilbo] used often to say there was only one Road; that it was like a great river: its springs were at every doorstep, and every path was its tributary. "It's a dangerous business, Frodo, going out of your door," he used to say. "You step into the Road, and if you don't keep your feet, there is no knowing where you might be swept off to." (1.83)

The assorted powers of evil are dedicated to sweeping all travelers off the one Road—not only into by-ways and ditches, but also into the pit of death. To know how to fight the good fight and to stay the course requires a knowledge of the Calamity that has marred the good creation, turning a symphony into a cacophony.

Chapter Two

The Calamity of Evil:
The Marring of the Divine Harmony

*T*olkien discloses both the complexity and subtlety of evil, never underestimating what is sinister about it. Yet he does not retell the biblical story of the Fall—not only because Milton and others have done it so well, but in order to ring fresh changes on the ancient problem of temptation and calamity. Tolkien has a profoundly Christian understanding of the nature of evil, even as he has a contemporary grasp on the terror it presents to our time. The aim of this chapter is to lay out the subtle logic of evil as it is revealed in *The Lord of the Rings* by looking at four of its chief manifestations: (1) how evil originates in the impatient desire for autonomy and independence; (2) how Sauron masters the elvish craft of metal work in order to fashion the Ring of total domination; (3) how this Ruling Ring binds Sauron's creatures by the ties of hatred and fear, causing them to destroy and consume each other, but only after they have first done enormous damage to the good; and also (4) how Sauron is immensely successful in seducing the Free Peoples with the three chief powers of the ring: longevity, invisibility, and coercion.

The Revolt of the Solitary Melkor

In *The Silmarillion*, we learn that six of the valar were created by Ilúvatar in pairs, and that they work together as virtual spouses. Yet three of the valar are single. Nienna, the sister of Manwë, is the very soul of suffering, one whose compassionate tears bring healing. Rather than encouraging those who suffer to languish in an endless grief, she calls them to spiritual endurance. Far from relishing her solitude, she dwells in intimate relationship with creatures other than herself. Ulmo is lord of waters and one of the chief architects in the making of Arda (the cosmos). He has learned more of Ilúvatar's music than any of the other valar, and he has also instructed the elves in the arts of harmony, even as he advises them through good dreams and the music of waters. Perhaps because he has no fixed dwelling place, Ulmo has no spouse. But his inspirational creativity gives him a constant concourse with others. Melkor ("He who arises in Might") exceeds all the other valar in power and knowledge. He is gifted by Ilúvatar with special talents in substances and crafts, but he uses these gifts to remain a solitaire subverter of Ilúvatar's purposes.

Everywhere in Tolkien, authentic existence is always communal—whether in dwarves or elves, wizards or hobbits or men, but also among the valar and maiar, and even for Ilúvatar himself. Here again Tolkien's vision is unabashedly biblical. Just as Adam could not be truly himself without Eve, so are all of the Hebrew patriarchs and matriarchs called by God—not to live in solitary faithfulness, but to serve as the progenitors of his people Israel. In Christian tradition, faithfulness always requires "two or more." Solitary fidelity is a contradiction in terms. Faithfulness is always communal. Jesus goes alone into the wilderness—just as Christian hermits still dwell in solitude—only for the sake of his community and Kingdom. Tolkien stands in full accord with this fundamental insistence that we become true persons only in engagement and community with other persons. He also discerns that pride, the deadliest of the cardinal sins, is usually a denial of our dependence on others. It is an attempt at pseudo-lordship—as if God himself were not a triune community of persons, as if he were not the God who refuses to be God without his people.

Melkor, by contrast, asks Friedrich Nietzsche's question: "If there were God, who could bear not to be God?" Yet he dared not be as honest as Nietzsche. Melkor was a deceiver about his godlike ambitions. He did not want it to be known that he despised everything he could not bring under his control—perhaps the sea most of all. Unlike the other two solitary valar who have good reason for remaining alone, Melkor seemed to have relished his isolation, until finally it became the excuse for his rebellion. He deprived himself of all communal reliance, even upon Ilúvatar. Thus did he grow impatient with the All-Father, refusing the proper call of sub-creation, wanting instead to create other beings on his own. He began to weave his own music into Ilúvatar's great symphony of creation. The result was an immense dissonance—so terrible, in fact, that the other valar were overwhelmed by Melkor's cacophony, and in their despondency they stopped their own song: "Then the discord of Melkor spread ever wider, and the melodies which had been heard before foundered in a sea of turbulent sound" (S, 16).

Melkor's brute noise was but the first of his many disturbances of Ilúvatar's good creation. Like Satan in Milton's epic, Melkor became jealous of the two unique races whom Ilúvatar made not through the valar, but through his own agency—namely, elves and men. Pretending to admire these new creatures—at first fooling even himself—Melkor set out to bring them under his own mastery so that, like Ilúvatar, he might be called Lord. Little does he understand that true lordship never coerces but always allures and invites. Melkor was also jealous that Ilúvatar alone possesses the Flame Imperishable, the Light of creative action. Yet unlike the generous All-Father, who shares this creative power, Melkor grasped it greedily unto himself:

> From splendour he fell through arrogance to contempt for all things save himself, a spirit wasteful and pitiless. Understanding he turned to subtlety in perverting to his own will all that he would use, until he became a liar without shame. He began with the desire of Light, but when he could not possess it for himself alone, he descended through fire and wrath into a great burning, down into Darkness. And darkness he used most in his evil works upon Arda, and filled it with fear for all living things. (S, 31)

The echoes here of the biblical Tempter—the subtlest beast of the field, the angel cast out of heaven, the father of lies, the one thrown into outer darkness, where there is weeping and wailing and gnashing of teeth—are unmistakable. Perhaps Melkor is most like Satan in forging for himself a crown of iron and thus according to himself a grandiose title, "King of the World" (S, 81). Yet Tolkien is careful to define the limits of even this most monstrous creature. Because Melkor rejects Ilúvatar's goodness, his iniquity has no real substance, no true right to exist, no proper being. Though frighteningly actual, the demonic always remains shadowy and derivative and in the deepest sense *unreal*. Tolkien has learned from St. Augustine that evil is *privatio boni*, the absence of good.

One of Tolkien's most important teachings is that we are never meant to take evil with the same seriousness that we accord to the Good, lest we become perversely fascinated with things we allegedly abominate. Such enthrallment would mark the ultimate triumph of evil. Hence Elrond's solemn warning against the mistake made by Saruman: "It is perilous to study too deeply the arts of the Enemy, for good or for ill" (1.278). We are not meant to stare at the Abyss lest, as Nietzsche warned, it stare back at us. It is crucial also to note that no Christian creed or confession declares, *Credo in diabolus*. Christians do not credit true being to the devil but to the triune God alone. We confess, instead, Christ's descent into Hell, while admitting that it too is a created realm—not an eternal reality. Tolkien wisely describes evil, therefore, as the Shadow: it is something secondary and derivative from the Light, not something primary and positive.

Tolkien demonstrates, exactly to the contrary, that sin is always a twisting and distortion and perversion of the Good. "Marring" is his favorite metaphor for the work of evil. It cannot destroy or undo goodness, but it can certainly tarnish and blight it. Since evil lives always as a parasite off the Good, the demonic Melkor was unable to produce any original or free creatures. He could manufacture only parodies and counterfeits. In addition to the carnivorous trolls that he bred in scorn for Ents, he has made the hideous orcs in mockery of elves. "The Shadow that bred [the orcs] can only mock," Frodo observes deep within the interior of Mordor, "it cannot make: not real new things of its own. I don't think it gave life to the orcs, it only ruined them and twisted them" (3.190).

The orcs serve both Melkor and Sauron in fear and hatred, not in loyalty—since evil must always coerce and enslave, never allowing free discipleship. Their works, even when crafty, are invariably malicious and destructive, as we learn in *The Hobbit*:

> Now [orcs] are cruel, wicked, and bad-hearted. They make no beautiful things, but they make many clever ones. They can tunnel and mine as well as any but the most skilled dwarves, when they take the trouble, though they are usually untidy and dirty. Hammers, axes, swords, daggers, pickaxes, tongs, and also instruments of torture, they make very well. . . . It is not unlikely that they invented some of the machines that have since troubled the world, especially the ingenious devices for killing large numbers of people at once. (H, 60)

Modern nuclear weapons are the obvious products of Melkor's latter-day disciples, as Tolkien brings home the demonic sources of our own culture of death. But ours is a far more vicious age than anything Middle-earth ever knew. Sauron's orcs decapitate their victims and throw the heads back over the fortress wall at Gondor, and we learn of the awful evils they inflicted on Gollum. Even so, Tolkien confessed that, if he had been writing an allegory of the modern world, he would have been compelled to make the hellish consequences of war much worse than they are in *The Lord of the Rings*: "The Ring would have been seized and used against Sauron; he would not have been annihilated but enslaved, and Barud-dûr [Sauron's fortress] would not have been destroyed but occupied" (1.7).

Yet Tolkien's epic does contain hints of the horrors perpetrated during World War II. Treebeard the Ent suggests that the terrible Uruk-hai are not merely an evil species of men made by Sauron, but rather the malevolent result of Sauron's cross-breeding of orcs and men. While these vicious warriors are frightful in their own right, wreaking awful mayhem at the Battle of Helm's Deep, the Uruk-hai also serve as fearful reminders that, about the same time Tolkien was writing his book, Nazi scientists were treating human life as a similarly malleable thing. They indulged in genetic matings that were prompted by a Sauronic desire to create a pure

Nordic race of supermen. The technology required for cloning these Blond Beasts was not available then as it is now, for surely it would have been used. Whenever we deny the fundamental dignity of human life as the unique and unalterable gift of God, Tolkien suggests, then such cruel and abominable experiments will surely result.

The wicked machinations of Melkor and Sauron make them enemies not only of the Free Peoples, but also of the faithful valar, who were forced to capture the greedy and vengeful Melkor. After a tumultuous struggle, they imprisoned him for three ages in the Halls of Mandos. Yet Melkor feigned repentance, chiefly through his silken language, and thus persuaded the compassionate Manwë to pardon and unchain him. Tolkien is candid about the guilelessness of the innocent before the deceptions of the wicked. Goodness, he suggests, is frightfully vulnerable to fraud: "Manwë was free from evil and could not comprehend it" (S, 65). Yet Tolkien also rejects the modern Faustian idea that knowledge and experience of evil are necessary for true virtue to flower. For Tolkien, evil will eventually reveal its sinister nature even to the ingenuous. The chicanery of Melkor was soon made evident to the faithful valar, as they had to subdue him once again. This time, however, he was cast permanently into the Void. There he will dwell until the End, when he will return to lead the forces of evil in the Dagor Dagorath, the Final Battle in which good will triumph.

The vile legacy of Melkor, alas, lives on. One of the main elven races, the Noldor, fell prey to his temptations. Of all the elves, the Noldor were most avid for learning and languages, for drawing and carving and the working of metal. Tolkien repeatedly demonstrates that evil often springs from the best of things rather than worst. *Corruptio optima pessima* (the corruption of the best is the worst) is an ancient maxim whose truth is also biblical: Peter the chief of the disciples is also the worst denier of his Lord. Thus did the Noldor elves' pride in their craftsmanship—especially in Fëanor's making of the Silmarils, the three magical jewels that possess ever-radiant light—lead them to become self-interested and ungrateful.

When one of the valar, Yavanna, asked Fëanor for the Silmarils in order to regrow the Two Trees destroyed by Ungoliant, he refused her. This act was not prompted by Melkor but by Fëanor's own selfishness—the perennial source of all evil. Yet it made Fëanor susceptible to Melkor's tempting claim that Ilúvatar had unfairly restricted the elves' creative freedom. Many of the Noldor elves thus refused Ilúvatar's command to remain in Valinor, there to reside in the earthly paradise created for them and the valar. They elected, instead, to go their own way. After Melkor stole the Silmarils to place them in his iron crown, Fëanor gave him a more sinister and appropriate name: the Morgoth ("the Dark Enemy"). Other elves swore a proud oath of fealty to Fëanor and so joined his pursuit of the fleeing Morgoth, as their path took them ever farther away from Valinor. For their refusal faithfully to occupy their proper place in Ilúvatar's good creation, these rebel Noldor were exiled to Middle-earth—though the penitent ones could return "diminished" to the Undying Lands.

Evil as Self-Devouring

Surely the worst legacy left by Morgoth was his seduction of various maiar into his cause. We are not told how many of them joined his revolt against Ilúvatar, but they include "the demons of terror" called the Balrogs. The most sinister of these recruits, however, is the maia called Sauron ("Abominable"). This evil one has risen "like a shadow of Morgoth and a ghost of his malice, and walked behind him on the same ruinous path down into the Void" (S, 32). Sauron has fought many battles against the valar, and he has ruined much of Ilúvatar's good creation. Yet he has also been defeated by the maia named Eönwë, the herald and standard-bearer for Manwë. Like Morgoth, Sauron agreed to repent of his evils, but his all-consuming pride would not allow him to enact such humility. Instead, he devised a new plan for subjecting the Free Peoples of Middle-earth to his will. Using his own skill, combined with the creativity of the Noldor elves whom he had inveigled, Sauron forged the gemstone Rings of Power: nine for men and seven for dwarves, though he did not make the three elven rings. All of these rings, far from being evil, enabled their wearers to accomplish immense good. Treacherously, however, Sauron also formed the plain gold band of the Ruling Ring. Into it he placed much of his own craft and power, including control over the nine rings designed for men.

Sauron has not always been successful in his war against the human species. Isildur, the elder son of Elendil, defeated him by cutting the Ring off Sauron's finger. Instead of destroying it, however, Isildur became mesmerized by its powers and refused to surrender the Ring. But in the Battle of Gladden Fields, it slipped off Isildur's finger and was lost in the River Anduin. There, many years later, it was found by a hobbit named Déagol. Here Tolkien's story takes on a clear resemblance to the account of Cain and Abel in the book of Genesis. Like Abel, whose sacrifice proved acceptable to God for no apparent reason, Déagol found the all-powerful Ring without any seeming merit of his own. Yet Déagol's friend Sméagol became intensely jealous of his comrade's good fortune. Like Cain, he was unable to accept his companion's serendipity, and thus murdered him to obtain the Ring. Rather than confessing his deadly greed, Sméagol now claims that the Ring was a birthday present that is deservedly his. Here Tolkien again demonstrates the seductive power of evil to overwhelm the truth, as those who commit sins and crimes must always justify them. Just as Adam blamed Eve for his own transgression, so does Sméagol transform his evil choice into a supposedly benign necessity. Seldom is sin committed for its own sake, Tolkien shows, but almost always in the name of some alleged good.

More lethal still, at least in the moral sphere, is the power of the Ring to destroy its owner's solidarity with others. Desperately determined to keep the Ring for himself, Sméagol has been cut off from all community, shunned by other hobbits, forced to live utterly unto himself. His movements are so primitive that he is hardly recognizable as a hobbit. He retches at the odor of freshly growing plants and herbs, and he despises *lembas*, the elven bread that possesses eucharistic airiness and thinness. Sméagol also refuses to eat cooked meat—thus denying the very rudiment of civilized life, the heated common meal. His possession of the Ring has so completely altered his character, in fact, that he is no longer called Sméagol but Gollum. His new name derives from his constant throat mutterings. Since he obsessively uses the Ring to catch and eat raw fish, Gollum has become entirely a creature of his appetite. His repetitive swallowing noises constitute his very identity, as Tolkien reveals that our personalities take on the quality of our acts. Outward behavior manifests inward convictions, whether for good or ill. "The good man out of the good treasure of his heart produces good, and the evil man out of his evil treasure produces evil; for out of the abundance of the heart his mouth speaks" (Luke 6:45).

Because evil has no substance of its own but lives parasitically off the good, Gollum forms a pseudo-community to replace the genuine engagement with others that he has abandoned. His throat-mumbling is the mark not only of his craving for fish but also of his constant chatter with himself. In his long possession of the Ring, Gollum has come to identify himself completely with it, not only calling it "My Precious," but also addressing himself with this same title. In fact, he always refers to himself with plural pronouns, as if he were two rather than one. So divisive is the effect of sin that it pits Gollum against himself. He becomes a literally duplicitous creature: he is doubled and utterly self-referential. The possessiveness engendered by the Ring also makes Gollum depersonalize others. He speaks of Frodo not in communal terms as "you" or "he" or "him," but as "it." Gollum first manifested this demeaning habit when Bilbo found the Ring, and then bested its former owner in the riddle contest. The furious Gollum asks Bilbo, "What has it got in its pocketses?" And when Bilbo flees, Gollum shouts this demeaning imprecation: *"Thief, thief! Baggins! We hates it forever!"* (1.22). Though Gollum occasionally calls him "master," Frodo is no longer a genuine "thou" to him—a fellow hobbit whom, even if he cannot love, he must respect and honor. Instead, he is a hated impersonal object.

Evil not only divides Gollum against himself, it also sets the disciples of Sauron against each other. The orcs who are slaves to Sauron are always quarreling among themselves. As these monstrous creatures snarl and snap at each other, they allow Merry and Pippin to escape. So is the renegade wizard Saruman also unable to enjoy true brotherhood with his chief lieutenant, Gríma (also called Wormtongue). Their mutual hostility becomes evident when they inadvertently surrender their *palantír*, the seeing stone with which they have been able to communicate with Sauron. Wormtongue flings it down in fury from the tower of Orthanc after Saruman fails to seduce Gandalf into employing the Ring for allegedly good ends. Nor is it altogether clear that Gríma was aiming at the wizard, as Aragorn explains to Gandalf: "The aim was poor, maybe, because he could not make up his mind which he hated more, you or Saruman" (2.189). Here Tolkien states, in indirect form, one of the deepest of Christian truths: all love that is not ordered to the love of God turns into hatred. Because Wormtongue has given his life in service to the corrupted wizard, he comes to despise him, and in the end Gríma slits Saruman's throat.

The mutual suspicion inherent in all coalitions of evil is also revealed when Pippin becomes so mesmerized by the *palantír* that he tries to handle it, only to expose himself to the vision of Sauron. The lord of all demons assumes that Pippin has been captured by Saruman and is being held captive in Orthanc—when, in fact, the *palantír* is now in possession of the Company. Yet even if Saruman confesses this calamity to Sauron, he is sure to be suspected of lying, since there is no trust to be found among the untrusting, as Gandalf declares:

> So Saruman will come to the last pinch of the vice that he has put his hand in. He has no captive to send. . . . Sauron will only believe that he is withholding the captive and refusing to use the Stone. It will not help Saruman to tell the truth. . . . So whether he will or no, he will appear a rebel. Yet he rejected us, so as to avoid that very thing! (2.205)

Though hardly cheering, the self-destructive character of evil is one of the hopes that Tolkien holds out to the Company. To console Pippin about the treachery of Gollum, Gandalf reminds him that "a traitor may betray himself and do good that he does not intend" (3.89). This small assurance that evil often undoes itself becomes especially important to the Fellowship, as it is gradually broken into small sub-communities of only two members each.

They remain tiny societies of the virtuous, while their enemies—
no matter how numerous or powerful—can never become communities of the vicious. King Théoden voices this odd confidence
in an apothegm: "*oft evil will shall evil mar*" (2.200). The life of
gangs and mobsters would appear to be a notable exception to this
rule, for these close-knit clans display immense loyalty to their
vision of the good—often surrendering their lives through acts of
terror committed against others. Yet even organized criminals are
known for their internecine life, as anyone who even whiffs of dis-
loyalty must be eliminated. Terrorist thugs are thus parodies of free
communities built on mutual trust: they are committed to sinister
aims rather than to purposes that are transcendently good.

No easy comfort can be found in the tendency of evil to devour
itself. Legolas seeks such solace when he discovers the bodies of
five slain orcs: "Enemies of the Orcs are likely to be our friends."
Aragorn corrects this naïve assumption by reminding the elf that
"the enemy brought his own enemy with him" (2.24). Orcs of one
kind are likely to attract another and even more vicious sort. So it
is with Sam and Frodo when they escape death in the tower of
Cirith Ungol because of orc strife. Frodo observes that such mutual
enmity must not be thought strange, since it "*is* the spirit of Mordor." Yet Frodo warns that "you can't get much hope" from evil's
self-destructiveness (3.203). It also destroys enormous good in the
process of consuming itself. Only great wisdom and even greater
patience—whether within the Company or among ordinary mor-
tals—can refuse the tactics of Sauron himself. Resorting to evil in
order to destroy evil would require a grotesque modification of
Théoden's motto: *oft "good" will shall "good" mar.*

Sauron's Eye and Galadriel's Mirror:
The Temptation of False Vision

When Sauron is finally defeated, we are told, he will never again
be perceived in bodily form. His kind of evil will have to resort,
instead, to far more sinister spiritual devices. Perhaps Sauron has
learned a lesson from his decision to assume physical existence.

Though his exact shape is uncertain, his only visible aspect is a gigantic lidless Eye. The eye is an organ of surfaces and appearances. At best, it gives information and knowledge, but neither discernment nor wisdom. As a singular Eye, moreover, Sauron lacks perspective and depth of vision. For all of his coercive might and expansive vision, he comprehends very little. He is completely lacking in sympathetic imagination—the power to enter other minds and other lives. The world of evil is absurd in the literal sense: *surdus* is Latin for "deaf." Sauron the Eye can hear nothing; he can receive no commands from Ilúvatar. In his all-seeing blindness, he dwells in the realm of unreason, chaos, absurdity. Sauron's metaphorical deafness also leaves him opaque to the selfless motives of the Company. As a demon who, already possessing immense power, seeks even greater might by means of his malice, Sauron cannot fathom Frodo's desire deliberately to surrender the Ring.

Tolkien does not naïvely honor the ear and hearing over the eye and seeing. At the entrance to Gondor, there are seats of both seeing and hearing. And when anyone wears the Ring, both hearing and sight are hugely increased. Yet there is little doubt about Tolkien's large regard for the heard word. His immense mastery of ancient tongues, his desire to speak and hear them spoken afresh, his love of the wisdom inherent in their speech—all these put him in fundamental accord with the biblical tradition. Israel's primary relation to God and the world is aural. Her very identity has an interlocutory character, as God's people are always asked to respond to his personal address. Whether God is speaking to Abraham or Moses, David or Elijah or Daniel, his Word comes as a call to obedience—usually to an action that turns the world utterly upside down. It is not surprising that Israel is prohibited from making images of Yahweh, for she is meant above all to hear and listen to him. A visible God would be an undeniable bully.

The high biblical regard for hearing is no happenstance. We can shutter ourselves to what is seen, having eyelids to seal off images and scenes that we do not want to behold. The ear, by contrast, has no flap for silencing unwanted voices. Earlobes are meant to increase hearing, not to prevent it. The ear is an organ for receiving declarations, and thus for either obeying or refusing commands. Obedience comes from the Latin *audire*, "to listen." Over and again Scripture declares that no one has seen God, while at the same time insisting that many have heard the word of God. Jesus himself offers an auditory more than a visual call: "He who has ears to hear, let him hear" (Matt. 11:15)—not "Let anyone with eyes, let him see." He also warns Thomas the Doubter against the naïve notion that seeing is believing: "Blessed are those who have not seen and yet believe" (John 20:29). Paul offers similar injunctions: "Now hope that is seen is not hope. For who hopes for what he sees? But if we hope for what we do not see, we wait for it with patience" (Rom. 8:24–25). Much of the Company's life consists in a patient waiting. As they wait, they spend much of their time in conversation—listening to stories of the past, receiving instruction from wise ones, learning of the hugely complex history that has intersected theirs.

Yet knowledge is no untrammeled good—unless the knower learns its limits. This again is a biblical truth, as witnessed in the second of the Genesis creation stories, where the lust for godlike knowledge leads to the Fall. Sam and Frodo learn that knowledge can be dangerous when they are allowed to peer into Galadriel's magical mirror. It is a basin of water that reveals things that are, that were, and that perhaps shall be—the present, the past, and the possible future. Such extraordinary vision would appear to be an enormous blessing. But to behold the future is especially dangerous. For if the foreseen future proves to be grim, the beholder may well despair. Sam and Frodo discover in fact that the prospect lying before them is terrifying. When Sam peers into the mirror, he beholds Frodo lying "dead" outside Shelob's Lair; he also foresees the later pillaging of the Shire by Saruman and his henchmen. Even full-blown knowledge of things present, especially of things evil, can be paralyzing, as when Frodo gets this chilling glimpse of Sauron himself:

> Frodo looked into emptiness. In the black abyss there appeared a single Eye that slowly grew, until it filled nearly all the Mirror. So terrible was it that Frodo stood rooted, unable to cry out

or to withdraw his gaze. The Eye was rimmed with fire, but was itself glazed, yellow as a cat's, watchful and intent, and the black slit of its pupil opened on a pit, a window into nothing. (1.379)

Evil is not something that truly exists, Tolkien profoundly discerns; it is nothing. Therein lies its real terror. If evil had a logical explanation, if it could be entirely explained as a perversion or distortion of the good, then it could be combated with considerable success. But because it is a devastating nothingness, a nameless black void, it possesses an irrationality that does not submit entirely to rational and moral control. As we have noticed, evil always has the character of absurdity. Sauron's power baffles understanding, prompts perplexity, and thus elicits despair. Despair is, in fact, the constant temptation of the Company—to give up, to quit, to surrender, to escape. When Sam and Frodo are shown their bleak future, they are tempted to turn back—as Tolkien suggests most people would do if they could look ahead to their own end. Yet the hobbits do not. Instead, they heed Galadriel's warning: "Remember that the Mirror shows many things, and not all have yet come to pass. Some never come to be, unless those that behold the visions turn aside from their path to prevent them" (1.378).

The Appeal of Evil to Virtue Even More than to Vice

The evil of self-righteousness is the vexing problem of both the Old and New Testaments. Repeatedly Israel is tempted to look with scorn upon her pagan neighbors because she takes false pride in being Yahweh's chosen and law-obedient people. Jesus castigates the Pharisees for their virtues rather than their vices: they are so fully compliant with divine law that they attribute their faithfulness to themselves rather than God. The problem is even more acute among Christians, who are prone to think that their holiness of life earns them honor before God. In his letters to the churches in both Rome and Galatia, Paul repeatedly inveighs against those who make their salvation in Christ an occasion for condemning others: "Therefore, you have no excuse, O man, whoever you are, when you judge another; for in passing judgment upon him you condemn yourself, because you, the judge, are doing the very same things" (Rom. 2:1). The Apostle makes a more positive appeal to the Galatians, though the warning against self-righteousness is the same: "Bear one another's burdens, and so fulfil the law of Christ. For if anyone thinks he is something, when he is nothing, he deceives himself" (Gal. 6:2–3).

Tolkien understands the odd danger posed by virtue cut off from the Good. Over and again, he demonstrates his fundamental conviction that evil preys upon our virtues far more than our vices. Our very strengths and assets—whether intelligence or bravery, diligence or loyalty or beauty, but especially righteousness—may dispose us either to scorn those who lack such virtues, or else to employ our gifts for our own selfish ends. Even Gandalf, the noblest of all the characters in *The Lord of the Rings*, is subject to such temptation. His outstanding virtue is pity, and he knows that it makes him the least capable bearer of the Ring. On the one hand, the Ring would give him the power to protect the weak so completely that they would never grow strong. On the other hand, the Ring's absolute power would enable him to forgive all evil, thus loosening the necessary tie between mercy and justice, pardon and repentance. Hence his vehement and fearful response to Frodo's offer of the Ring:

> "No!" cried Gandalf, springing to his feet. "With that power I should have power too great and terrible. And over me the Ring would gain a power still greater and more deadly." His eyes flashed and his face was lit as by a fire within. "Do not tempt me! For I do not wish to become like the Dark Lord himself. Yet the way of the Ring to my heart is by pity, pity for weakness and the desire of strength to do good. Do not tempt me! I dare not take it, not even to keep it safe, unused. The wish to wield it would be too great for my strength. I shall have such need of it. Great perils lie before me." (1.70–71)

The elven princess Galadriel suffers a similar temptation when she is offered the Ring. She has done much to redeem the infidelity of her Noldor people. She has also befriended the Company with the elven cloaks, the waybread, and other gifts that enable their very survival. The phial that she gives to Frodo, containing some of the original light belonging to the Silmarils and the Two Trees, helps him and Sam make their way in the infernal darkness of Shelob's Lair. Even so, Galadriel's remarkable beauty and holiness expose her to unique temptation. She could become deadly in her beauty—a prospect that late modernity, with its virtual worship of gorgeousness, can scarcely comprehend.

Tolkien expressed alarm, in fact, that our world finds "it difficult to conceive of evil and beauty together. The fear of the beautiful fay [fairy] that ran through the elder ages almost eludes our grasp. Even more alarming: goodness is itself bereft of its proper beauty" (MC, 151). As in the biblical understanding of angels, so are elves to be feared for their very goodness. Thus does the good and beautiful Galadriel confess that she too has pondered the possibility of seizing the Ring. It would enable her to realize her long-held desire to rule independently, a lust first aroused by the rebel elf Fëanor. Frodo's offer of the Ring thus represents for Galadriel the supreme test:

> I do not deny that my heart has greatly desired to ask what you offer. For many long years I had pondered what I might do, should the Great Ring come into my hands, and behold! it was brought within my grasp. The evil that was devised long ago works on in many ways, whether Sauron himself stands or falls. Would not that have been a noble deed to set to the credit of his Ring, if I had taken it by force or fear from my guest? (1.381)

Like Faramir and Sam—but unlike Boromir and Saruman—Galadriel is able to refuse the Ring's magnetic lure. Bilbo had also used the Ring many times without permanent damage. Whence the difference? Why can some resist the fatal temptation while others yield to it? Boromir and Saruman both see themselves as leaders and heroes; their loves are disordered by their own lust and ambition. The others, by contrast, possess something akin to what Jesus calls purity of heart (Matt. 5:8). They have preserved their integrity of soul and conscience. They regard themselves as servants rather than lords. All four of them have properly ordered their loves to the Good. Bilbo lives to write his books and poems, and to translate works from the elvish for the benefit of hobbits. Sam serves his master Frodo above all others. Faramir seeks to preserve Gondor in readiness for the king's return. Galadriel wants only to protect Lórien from the assaults of the evil one. Because their loves and thus their lives are rightly ordered, the Ring does them little harm.

Since the Ring would seemingly aid Galadriel in this task—her great strength being insufficient to defend Lórien against Sauron—she has far greater potential for corruption than either hobbits or men. And so she must repudiate it in the firmest terms. If she possessed its coercive power, she confesses, her loveliness would become binding rather than inviting. Everyone would bow down and adore her beauty, subjecting their wills to hers—thus putting an end to all liberty and true beauty. Hence her stern response to the offer of the Ring:

> And now at last it comes. You will give me the Ring freely! In place of the Dark Lord you will set up a Queen. And I shall not be dark, but beautiful and terrible as the Morning and the Night! Fair as the Sea and the Sun and the Snow upon the Mountain! Dreadful as the Storm and the Lightning! Stronger than the foundations of the earth. All shall love me and despair! (1.381)

Just as Morgoth had refused Ilúvatar's communal harmony in favor of his own his solitary music, so would Galadriel have come to preside over a crowd of slaves, not a community of souls. She would have become a new and worse Sauron. Instead, she becomes an ever more admirable servant of the Quest. Frodo has spied the ring on her finger as Nenya, one of the three elven rings. It has kept Lórien safe from Sauron's depredations. Even so, if Frodo fails to destroy the Ruling Ring, Sauron will surely invade and conquer the elven realm. What makes Galadriel such a remarkable figure is her serenity amidst the coming defeat of her realm and her people. Far from resigning herself to any sort of fatalism, she desires only that the *ought* shall become the *is*:

> "Yet if you [Frodo] succeed, then our power is diminished, and Lothlórien will fade, and the tides of Time will sweep it away. We must depart into the West, or dwindle to a rustic folk of dell and cave, slowly to forget and to be forgotten."

Frodo bent his head. "And what do you wish?" he said at last. "That what should be shall be," she answered. "The love of the Elves for their land and their works is deeper than the deeps of the Sea, and their regret is undying and cannot ever wholly be assuaged. Yet they will cast all away rather than submit to Sauron: for they know him now." (1.380)

The power of evil to subvert virtue is not as readily resisted in others as it is in Galadriel. Boromir, for example, is indeed a valiant man, a warrior imbued with the virtue of courage. He fears not death from Sauron's forces. On the contrary, he insists that the Company employ the Ring against Sauron in order to defeat him—unlike the deceiving Saruman, who urges them to use it in alleged cooperation with Sauron. Thus does Boromir display a bravado that is also blind. His sight is also dimmed by his despair at knowing that Gondor does not have troops sufficient to defend itself against an all-out assault from Mordor. The only hope seems thus to lie in a valiant assault on Sauron himself by means of the Ring.

Boromir fails to discern the indivisibility of the virtues. One cannot be truly courageous without also being imbued with wisdom and justice and temperance and the other virtues. In Christian tradition, moreover, the ancient virtue of *courage*—the willingness to kill in defense of the good, even if it means one's own death—becomes radically transformed into the new virtue of *martyrdom*: the willingness to make one's witness by being killed rather than denying one's faith in order to remain alive. Such is the witness the Fellowship will make at the battle of Pelennor Fields, where they will maintain their faith in the Quest by facing Sauron's armies like lambs led to the slaughter.

Boromir wants to die, if he must, a heroic death above all else. He is unable to discern that his great valor would be corrupted by his possession of the Ring. Even if he were to defeat Sauron by using the Ring in all-out direct combat, Boromir would then become (as both Galadriel and Gandalf have warned) a new and worse Lord of Darkness. Blind to such ironies, Boromir tries to seize the Ring from Frodo. The hobbit, in turn, is forced to put on the Ring in order to escape one of his own companions. So sinister is the power of evil to corrupt virtue that the Fellowship is broken from within rather than without, by a friend rather than a foe—not by Saruman or the Ringwraiths, but by their own companion Boromir, who acts in the name of heroic bravery:

> True-hearted Men, they will not be corrupted [by the Ring]. We of Minas Tirith have been staunch through long years of trial. We do not desire the power of wizard-lords, only strength to defend ourselves, strength in a just cause. And behold! in our need chance brings to light the Ring of Power. It is a gift, I say; a gift to the foes of Mordor. It is mad not to use it, to use the power of the Enemy against him. The fearless, the ruthless, these alone will achieve victory. What could not a warrior do in this hour, a great leader? What could not Aragorn do? Or if he refuses, why not Boromir? The Ring would give me power of Command. How I would drive the hosts of Mordor, and all men would flock to my banner! (1.414)

The logic of Boromir's argument reveals that his courage is already corrupted. He begins by wanting valiantly to defeat Sauron, then he hails not the heroic warrior so much as the merciless killer, but only to promote himself as the rightful wielder of the Ring, and finally to acclaim the glory that would accrue to him alone—as his speech ends in a sputter of personal references.

The Lure of Longevity and the Longing for Invisibility

One of the chief allurements of the Ring is that it gives its bearer ongoing life. Gollum has borne it the longest of any mortal creature in Middle-earth, and as a result his existence has been tremendously prolonged: he is very old. Yet with his increase in quantity of years, Gollum has received no increase in quality of life. On the contrary, he has been nearly consumed by the Ring. He is emaciated both physically and spiritually because his imagination has been turned entirely upon himself in a self-consuming satisfaction of his own desires. Yet Gandalf's description of him reveals that, for all that is sinister in this twisted creature, Gollum is more pathetic than despicable. Evil punishes itself, for its disordered love turns into secret hatred of the very thing it idolizes, as Gandalf explains:

> All the "great secrets" under the mountains had turned out [for Gollum] to be just empty night: there was nothing more to find out, nothing worth doing, only nasty furtive eating and resentful remembering. He was altogether wretched. He hated the dark, and he hated light more: he hated everything, and the Ring most of all. . . . He hated it and loved it, as he hated and loved himself. (1.64)

For Tolkien, the modern obsession with quantity rather than quality of life is the mark of our unbelief. To be obsessed with prolonging our existence well beyond the bounds of our allotted biblical years is to worship life rather than the God of life. Someone has said that, if asked about the chief purpose of human existence, many denizens of the modern West would reply, if they could muster the candor: "It is to stay alive, not to die, and the purpose of staying alive is to have a good time." Our only commonality is the fear of death. Hence the burgeoning power of the health and amusement industries as, virtually around the clock, most citizens of the so-called "developed" countries are either being entertained or receiving one kind of therapy or another. Whereas medieval cities were focused on cathedrals, ours are built around our huge medical complexes, even as our suburbs have country clubs and golf courses at their center. In this mania for longevity and pleasure, Tolkien shows that we have lost the ancient honesty of the psalmist: "So teach us to number our days that we may get a heart of wisdom" (90:12). As we shall see, he regards death as one of our greatest gifts.

The Ruling Ring provides a temptation altogether as seductive as longevity—namely, invisibility. To put on the Ring is to disappear from sight, at least from all but Sauron and his Ringwraiths. Oddly, it cannot block the vision of the pure—namely, of those who have lived in the Undying Lands. The Ring's power of invisibility proves helpful to both Bilbo and Frodo, who escape their pursuers while wearing it. Yet here the Ring serves to enable the Quest only unintentionally. On the whole, Tolkien suggests that it is evil to be granted never-ending life and the absence of visible, outward existence. These two "gifts" have utterly ruined Gollum, as he has repeatedly used the Ring to indulge his obsessive appetite for raw fish.

Tolkien no doubt knew Plato's account, in the *Republic*, of Gyges' magical ring with the power to make its wearer invisible. Glaucon recounts the myth in order to refute Socrates' argument that the doing of good needs no external threat or reward. Goodness is so inherently satisfying, Socrates insists, that it requires no compensation. Glaucon contends, on the contrary, that the story of Gyges demonstrates what happens when human nature is not constrained. For with his magical ring, Gyges was able to get anything he wanted. He could steal and kill without being caught; he could seduce the king's wife by getting into her bed without her knowing it; he could even kill the king and ascend the throne himself—all by means of his invisibility. Tolkien the Christian understands our fallen human nature as Plato the rationalist did not, and he is much more agreed with Glaucon than Socrates. Gollum is his non-Platonic witness to the seductive strength of evil when it manifests itself through the occult power of invisibility.

The Coercive Power of the One Ring

Even when Sauron is not at hand, luring both the sinister gold band and its keeper to himself, the Ring has the power to tempt Frodo. For in wearing it, he can escape immediate threats and thus preserve his own life, even if not the lives of his friends. The evil deed is able always to justify itself, as in Frodo's early desire to use the Ring to escape the Barrow-wights: "He thought of himself running free over the grass, grieving for Merry, and Sam, and Pippin, but free and alive himself. Gandalf would admit that there had been nothing else he could do" (1.152). Frodo resists this initial temptation, and his resistance to its powers grows with every denial. Yet the Ring's coercive pressure continues to bear down on him, ever more as an external force that he must refuse, ever less as an internal longing for his own relief.

There is no doubt that corporeal life can become a great weariness—whether from illness or age or even the troubles of the mind and spirit—so much so, in fact, that it is tempting simply to be rid of one's body. Sometimes the elves are so grieved that their spirits simply flee their bodies. But it is the Ring's wearying effects that make Bilbo tired of life. He confesses to Gandalf that, though he still seems vigorous, he nonetheless feels "all thin, sort of *stretched*, if you know what I mean: like butter that has been scraped over too much bread" (1.41). The Ring has given Bilbo quantity but not quality of life. No wonder, then, that its ruination of Gollum is so great. Since he possessed the Ring for five hundred years, he has regressed to an almost infantile, animal-like state.

Though he has borne the Ring for a comparatively short while, Frodo is quickly wearied by it. He is tempted to put on the Ring in order to escape the burden of evil, though it will enable Sauron and his minions to locate and devour him. Even an uninviting distant relative such as Lobelia Sackville-Baggins can tempt Frodo to wear the Ring. "Honestly," Frodo explains to Gandalf, "I nearly tried on Bilbo's ring. I longed to disappear" (1.48). But usually it is the pressing power of the Ring itself that makes him want simply to vanish, perhaps into nothingness. This temptation becomes especially acute as he faces the Ringwraiths: "[S]omething seemed to be compelling him to disregard all warnings, and he longed to yield. Not with the hope of escape, or doing anything, either good or bad: he simply felt that he must take the Ring and put it on his finger" (1.207–8).

The essence of the Ring's evil is coercion as well as seduction: it enslaves the will. Not even Gandalf can break its power, nor does he desire to do so. Only if Frodo freely surrenders and destroys the Ring in the volcanic Cracks of Doom can his own mind and will be freed from its compulsion. Gandalf explains the deep and paradoxical relation between freedom and the good, as also between coercion and evil: "Already you too, Frodo cannot easily let it go, nor will to damage it. And I could not 'make' you—except by force, which would break your mind" (1.70). For Gandalf magically to have liberated Frodo from the Ring's constraints would have made the hobbit into Gandalf's puppet. Yet the alternative is almost as evil, for with his every refusal of the Ring's magnetic power, it bears down on Frodo ever more irresistibly.

Tolkien is close to Paul and Augustine and their long train of followers who argue that real freedom is the liberty to choose and do the good, and that to do evil is to act unfreely, to exercise an enslaved will. These theologians all insist that God's grace *enables* our right response to it. For this venerable theological tradition, it is better to say that we are the product of the gifts we have graciously received rather than the sum of the decisions we have bravely made. Not all evil is chosen. For while evil can subtly seduce, it can also brutally enforce its will. When the Ring thus bullies its victims, it can work its spell on even the most resistant will. This is the bitter truth that Frodo discovers in the Company's first encounter with the Ringwraiths:

> Frodo was hardly less terrified than his companions; he was quaking as if he was bitter cold, but his terror was swallowed up in a sudden temptation to put on the Ring. The desire to do this laid hold of him, and he could think of nothing else. . . . He could not speak. He felt Sam looking at him, as if he knew that his master was in some trouble, but he could not turn towards him. . . . He shut his eyes and struggled for a while; but resistance became unbearable, and at last he slowly drew out the chain, and slipped the Ring on the forefinger of his left hand. (1.207–8)

As the Company and their friends move ever closer to their final confrontation with Sauron and his mighty forces, they are required to exercise their own wills to defy the onslaught of evil. Some of them seem to resist it more readily than others. Faramir confesses, for instance, that he would not pick up the Ring if he found it lying by the road, and Sam is able to relinquish it freely. Yet Tolkien repeatedly emphasizes the power of the Ring to break even the strongest of wills. Gandalf warns Boromir, for example, that "its strength . . . is too great for anyone to wield at will, save only those who have already a great power of their own. But for them it holds an even deadlier peril. The very desire of it corrupts the heart" (1.281).

Precisely by such desire is Boromir corrupted. Even had he succeeded in seizing the Ring from Frodo, Boromir would have used the Ring as he promised—to fight and perhaps even to defeat Sauron. But then he would have exalted himself as a new and worse Lord of Evil. Gandalf explains the coercive power of the Ring to Denethor, the father of Boromir: "He would have stretched out his hand to this thing, and taking it he would have fallen. He would have kept it for his own, and when he returned you would not have known your son" (3.86). The Ring creates a compulsion, in short, that cannot be broken with mere human strength of will. Tolkien gives new and chilling credence to the saying of Lord Acton: "Absolute power corrupts absolutely."

Frodo himself, as bearer of the Ring, finds its force to be increasingly irresistible. So it was with Bilbo. His frivolous use of the Ring at his going-away birthday party seems but a mischievous prank. When Gandalf returns to take the Ring from him, however, Bilbo has become surprisingly entranced by it. In fact, the wizard is forced to threaten Bilbo with wrath before the hobbit will surrender it. Even in his dotage, when Frodo and the Company come to visit the doddering Bilbo in Rivendell, the old hobbit still lusts for the Ring—so great is its mesmerizing control over him. Even guileless Sam feels the compulsion of the Ring when he takes it from the seemingly dead Frodo outside Shelob's Lair. He finds his hand moving inexorably toward the Ring, as if his own body had been autonomously inhabited by its power. Sam is able to refuse the Ring's lure largely because his heart is uncorrupted, because he desires nothing other than to serve his master Frodo, and because his guilelessness penetrates the deceits of the Enemy in the tower of Cirith Ungol:

> Wild fantasies arose in his mind; and he saw Samwise the Strong, Hero of the Age, striding with a flaming sword across the darkened land, and armies flocking to his call as he marched to the overthrow of Barad-dûr. And then all the clouds rolled away, and the white sun shone, and at his command the vale of Gorgoroth became a garden of flowers and trees and brought forth fruit. He had only to put on the Ring and claim it for his own, and all this could be.
>
> In that hour of trial it was the love of his master that helped

most to hold him firm; but also deep down in him lived still unconquered his plain hobbit-sense: he knew in the core of his heart that he was not large enough to bear such a burden, even if such visions were not a mere cheat to betray him. The one small garden of a free gardener was all his need and due, not a garden swollen to a realm; his own hands to use, not the hands of others to command. (3.177)

Frodo's will, by contrast, is overwhelmed by the commanding power of the Ring. The closer he comes to the place where it was forged in the very heart of Sauron's evil empire, the greater its power over him. It has not only rendered Frodo physically emaciated; it has also drained his spirit, leaving him with an overwhelming sense of hopelessness. The dread fear that he will not succeed in his mission, especially as the obstacles to his errand increase in fury and horror, infects Frodo with a deep pessimism. The Ring begins to occupy every waking moment of Frodo's consciousness: "I begin to see it in my mind all the time, like a great wheel of fire. . . . I am naked in the dark, Sam, and there is no veil between me and the wheel of fire. I begin to see it even with my waking eyes, and all else fades" (3.196, 215).

Having repeatedly shown pity to the treacherous Gollum and having arrived at the Cracks of Doom so weary that he cannot walk, Frodo seems incapable of self-defense, much less self-will. But when Gollum leaps on Frodo's back in an attempt to seize the Ring at the last, Frodo flicks him away as if he were an insect. Sam is rightly startled to find Frodo suddenly so strong and merciless. It is evident that Frodo has mustered a heroic determination to carry out his Quest at the absolute end. So fully is he imbued with both sanctity and strength that Frodo undergoes a virtual transfiguration. Sam sees him, therefore, as a stern and terrible creature, "untouchable now by pity, a figure robed in white" (3.221). At the very apogee of Frodo's holiness and might, however, he is overwhelmed by Sauronic force. Frodo becomes, in fact, a virtual ventriloquist for the coercive evil that invades both his mind and will, as he speaks in a loud and stentorian voice that is not at all his own: "I have come," Frodo declares. "But I do not choose now to do

what I came to do. I will not do this deed. The Ring is mine!"
(3.223).

This is surely the most surprising and anti-climactic moment in
the novel. After his long twilight struggle to carry the Ring back to
the Cracks of Doom, Frodo fails at the very last—not because of
his own weakness of will but because the Ring finally overwhelms
him. Thus does the Quest end not in jubilant victory but disap-
pointing defeat, as Tolkien deflates all his readers' hopes for a conventional heroic ending. Yet he accomplishes something far more
important—the awful juxtaposition of radical good and radical
evil. Tolkien demonstrates that the mightiest evil can summon
forth the very highest good in a character such as Frodo, even as it
defeats him. So did Gethsemane end in Golgotha, as Jesus died
with a shout that is hardly a cry of conquest. The cross is the great
Christian eucatastrophe because it is sheer defeat overcome by
sheer victory.

The Quest is completed not by Frodo the brave but by the greed-
maddened Gollum as he bites the Ring off Frodo's finger and,
dancing his jig of joy at the brink of the volcanic fissure, tumbles
with it into the inferno. Sauron's voice had warned Gollum that he
would go to the fire if he seized the Ring. Yet the prophecy is fulfilled in ways that neither of them could have foreseen, as the Ring
finally destroys itself. Many readers have been flattened by this
conclusion to the Quest. They have wanted Frodo to act heroically
at the end, flinging the Ring triumphantly into the molten lava that
alone can dissolve it. Such an ending would have provided us with
a traditional hero whom we could have exalted and acclaimed as
one of our own. It would have also assured us that evil can be
defeated by dint of human and hobbitic effort.

Tolkien refuses such illusions. By granting the Ring the power
of coercion, Tolkien uncovers what is surely the chief evil of the
modern world—the various tyrannies that have been exercised
over the human spirit. The most obvious examples are to be found
in the assorted totalitarianisms of the previous century. Quite apart
from the multiplied millions who were slaughtered by their own
governments, many more were made to live in constant fear of vio-
lating the oppressive system and thus bringing its terror upon them.

Theirs was the daily dread that the Company also must eat. Tolkien demonstrates that the human spirit is not meant to bear up under such hideous pressures. Yet we who live in the so-called free world—the nations of the democratic West—have created our own compulsions. Our culture of comfort and convenience offers allurements altogether as personally enslaving as totalitarian regimes are politically imprisoning. Yet *The Lord of the Rings* envisions a drastically alternative way of life that is dedicated to overcoming the siren charms and coercions of evil. And it is to this human counter-action and divine corrective to the calamity of evil that we now turn.

Chapter Three

The Counter-Action to Evil:
Tolkien's Vision of the Moral Life

*T*olkien's engagement with evil in *The Lord of the Rings*, though fearfully honest and utterly convincing, is not the heart of his book. This would be true only if he had confined himself to its pagan and pre-Christian ethos. While Tolkien immensely admired the heroic cultures of ancient Scandinavia and Germany, he could not finally affirm the overwhelming darkness and hopelessness of their outlook. In the antique pagan world, evil could be resisted but not overcome, either in this life or the next. As we have heard from the Venerable Bede, life in the antique North was likened to the flight of a sparrow into the one end of a lighted mead hall and out the other: from black nothingness into brief light and then back to final night. For all the honor that Tolkien accords to the grim realism of Northernness, he was a devout Catholic who infused his work with profound Christian convictions. The chief of these convictions is that the Light defines the darkness, that evil's triumph is not final, that even within this present life it can be partially overcome, that true life is animated by a true vision of the finally triumphant Good, and therefore that we have been given a wondrous means of counter-action to the calamity that Melkor and Sauron and their slaves have brought into the world.

The perennial appeal of Tolkien's great novel lies in this bright vision of hope, and thus in the moral and religious strength that it yields. Many of my students have confessed that they feel "clean" after reading *The Lord of the Rings*. They refer not chiefly to the book's avoidance of decadent sex but, far more significantly, to its bracing moral power: its power to lift them out of the small-minded obsessions of the moment and into the perennial concerns of ethical and spiritual life.

Yet while Tolkien made *The Lord of the Rings* implicitly Christian as *The Silmarillion* is not, this change is not won at the expense of the pagan virtues. Knowing that the early church made common cause with the best qualities of its surrounding cultures—especially their moral teaching—Tolkien follows this ancient Christian practice. He shares the sentiment of Augustine that Christians should raid the treasures of the pagans just as the Israelites brought gold out of Egypt. Only when the virtues are related strictly to themselves and not referred to God, says Augustine, do they become vices. Hence Tolkien's insistence that Christians have no right to despise even so despairing a theme as the one that pervades *Beowulf*—"that man, each man and all men, and all their works shall die. . . . that all glory (or as we might say 'culture' or 'civilization') ends in night" (MC, 23).

Tolkien held with both Augustine and Aquinas that Christian revelation completes and perfects human knowledge and effort. Since he was a Catholic who subscribed to the synthesis of pagan and Christian thought forged by these great medieval theologians, we will examine his understanding of the moral life by examining the four classical or cardinal virtues—prudence, justice, fortitude, and temperance. They enable human existence to flourish, in an elementary but indispensable way, even apart from the revelation given in Israel and Christ. Yet it is important to emphasize that all human longings and possibilities are already the gift of God. "You have made us for yourself," St. Augustine famously declares at the beginning of his *Confessions*, "and our hearts are restless until they rest in You." The so-called pagan virtues are not autonomous human achievements, therefore, but the work of God's grace already and always present in human life.

Because the virtues are divinely implanted, the moral life is not a program of ethical uplift, strenuous self-help, or a determined striving to do better. As Augustine makes clear, we have to be made teachable by God's own grace: "Whence it happens that even with the assistance of holy men, or even if the holy angels themselves take part, no one rightly learns those things which pertain to life with God unless he is made by God docile to God, to whom it is said in the Psalm, 'teach me to do thy will, for thou art my God'" (*On Christian Doctrine*, 4.33). When thus infused with divine grace, the cardinal virtues are not only enabled but transformed. They are stretched beyond ordinary human potential to achieve things transcendently good. Again according to Augustine, they become the very basis of the Christian life:

> To live well is nothing other than to love God with all one's heart, with all one's soul and with all one's efforts; from this it comes about that love is kept whole and uncorrupted (through temperance). No misfortune can disturb it (and this is fortitude). It obeys only [God] (and this is justice), and is careful in discerning things, so as not to be surprised by deceit or trickery (and this is prudence). (*On the Morals of the Catholic Church*, 1, 25, 46)

Tolkien the Christian imbues *The Lord of the Rings* not only with the pagan virtues as they are classically conceived, but also with the conviction that, when completed and perfected, prudence issues in holy folly, justice in undeserved mercy, courage in unexpected endurance, and temperance in joyful self-denial.

Wisdom and Prudence:
The Virtues That Prompt Self-Sacrifice

Gandalf's very name indicates his gift of wisdom. "Wizard" derives from the Middle English *wys*, meaning wise. The proper name for wizards in Tolkien's mythology is Istari, which means "scholars." Gandalf's wisdom is thus linked to his learning. Wisdom is also a central virtue in the biblical tradition. Both Proverbs and Ecclesiastes speak of the wise as being receptive to instruction, as heeding the counsel of others, as possessing self-control, honesty, diligence. The restraint and integrity of the wise enable them to act in a timely way, so that wisdom becomes a practical as well as an intellectual virtue. The wise are also teachers and scholars and writers, and they are usually old, like Gandalf, since their wisdom has been gained from long experience. The opposite of the wise man is the fool: the one so driven by passions and false desires as to act wrongly. Gandalf calls Saruman a "fool" (2.188) in this precise sense. The fool finally is driven to deny even God: "The fool says in his heart, 'There is no God'" (Ps. 14:1). While the Old Testament derives wisdom from God's good creation, the New Testament locates it in Jesus Christ himself. He is a rabbi, a wisdom teacher. Jesus employs the aphoristic and parabolic style of the sages, and he invites his disciples to "learn from me" (Matt. 11:29). Paul also exalts wisdom. He commands Christians to "walk, not as unwise men but as wise" (Eph. 5:15), and to receive the "spirit of wisdom" from the Father of glory (Eph. 1:17).

The classical virtue of prudence is not far removed from the biblical understanding of wisdom. Yet the word "prudence" has been corrupted almost beyond retrieval. We have come to think of prudential people as small-minded seekers after their own self-preservation. For the ancient Greeks and Romans, by contrast, prudence was the chief of the virtues, the one on which all the others are based. It informs the other virtues because it entails a clear-eyed knowledge of objective truth as well as the ability to act on this knowledge. The prudent person makes decisions that are appropriate to the particular situation. Aragorn is a fit ruler and future king of Gondor and Arnor because he possesses wisdom and prudence of this kind. Repeatedly he helps the Company deal with true dilemmas—not with choices between good and evil, but between equally uninviting alternatives.

Aragorn displays his prudence perhaps most clearly when the Company is first divided, with Frodo and Sam fleeing toward Mordor, while Merry and Pippin have been captured by orcs. It would seem obvious that he should seek to aid the Ring-bearer and Sam, but Aragorn's wisdom discerns not the patent but the subtle truth—that they should rescue the weakest of the hobbits:

> "Let me think!" said Aragorn. "And now may I make a right choice, and change the evil fate of this unhappy day!" He stood silent for a moment. "I will follow the Orcs," he said at last. "I

would have guided Frodo to Mordor and gone with him to the end; but if I seek him now in the wilderness, I must abandon the captives to torment and death. My heart speaks clearly at last: the fate of the Bearer is in my hands no longer. The Company has played its part. Yet we that remain cannot forsake our companions while we have strength left. Come! We will go now. Leave all that can be spared behind! We will press on by day and dark!" (2.21)

Aragorn's appeal to the dictates of his heart reveals that prudence is a virtual synonym for conscience. The heart is the locus of desire, and the chest has been understood as the traditional stronghold of conscience—no less than the place of its worst violations. "The precepts of the LORD are right, rejoicing the heart" (Ps. 19:8). "The heart is deceitful above all things, and desperately corrupt; who can understand it?" (Jer. 17:9). The heart must be transfigured by prudence and wisdom in order for the desires to be redirected toward the Good. Only when the conscience is properly formed can we instinctively discern the truth and act swiftly upon it.

Tolkien's adherence to the classical Christian understanding of education as "training in virtue" accounts for the long chapters devoted to the learning of ancient lore, as the Company listens to the stories and legends that give moral and spiritual shape to their lives. The second chapters of the first two books of *The Fellowship of the Ring*—"The Shadow of the Past" and "The Council of Elrond"—serve not as mere historical background, but rather as carefully narrated wisdom. We encounter prudential wisdom at many other places in Tolkien. Aphorisms—succinctly expressed wisdom distilled from the long human struggle— occur throughout *The Lord of the Rings*. *"Need brooks no delay, yet late is better than never"* (3.110). *"Twice blessed is help unlooked for"* (3.123). *"Oft hope is born, when all is forlorn"* (3.153). *"Too often seen is seen no longer"* (MR, 316). Sometimes these chestnut apothegms have to be modified. When finally the Shire is cleansed of its invaders and thus restored to its original happiness, old Gaffer Gamgee exclaims: "All's well as ends Better!" (3.302). The compressed wisdom that counts most is also rhymed:

All that is gold does not glitter,
Not all those who wander are lost;
The old that is strong does not wither,
Deep roots are not reached by the frost,
From the ashes a fire shall be woken,
A light from the shadows shall spring;
Renewed shall be blade that was broken:
The crownless again shall be king.
(1.260–61)

The Consequences of Imprudence in Matters of Renown and Romance

To lack prudence and wisdom is to act foolishly and thoughtlessly—seeking merely one's own good rather than the good of friends and the larger community. Tolkien deftly discloses such imprudence at work in the otherwise admirable character of Éowyn. She chafes at the restrictions that her gender has forced upon her. She does not want to be relegated to the role of protector and steward in the absence of King Théoden and his warriors. She possesses the bravery of even the most valiant man, and she wants it to be fully realized and recognized in her role as shieldmaiden:

"Your duty is with your people," [Aragorn] answered.
"Too often have I heard of duty," [Éowyn] cried. "But am I not of the House of Eorl, a shieldmaiden and not a dry-nurse? I have waited on faltering feet long enough. Since they falter no longer, it seems, may I not now spend my life as I will?"
"Few may do that with honour," he answered. . . .
"Shall I always be left behind when the Riders depart, to mind the house while they win renown, and find food and beds when they return?"
"A time may come soon," said he, "when none will return. Then there will be need of valour without renown, for none shall remember the deeds that are done in the last defence of your homes. Yet the deeds will not be less valiant because they are unpraised."
And she answered: "All your words are but to say: you are a

woman, and your part is in the house. But when the men have died in battle and honour, you have leave to be burned in the house, for the men will need it no more. But I am of the House of Eorl and not a serving-woman. I can ride and wield blade, and I do not fear either pain or death."

"What do you fear, lady?" [Aragorn] asked.

"A cage," she said. "To stay behind bars, until use and old age accept them, and all chance of doing great deeds is gone beyond recall or desire." (3.57–58)

A contemporary feminist could hardly make a more impassioned case for the liberation of women from their traditional roles, and Tolkien is evidently sympathetic. Yet Éowyn reveals her imprudence in ways that must be remarked. She lusts after renown. She believes that her only lasting worth lies in being remembered for her brave deeds, especially in dying heroically while defending her people. Tolkien does not set up Éowyn as an easy target for criticism. In her urgency to seek satisfaction in present celebrity and future fame, she stands in accord with many ancient and modern cultures—especially those which lack any transcendent moral or religious referent.

Aragorn answers Éowyn's plea in terribly unfashionable terms that Tolkien makes no attempt to soften. Aragorn reminds this fearless lady that her vocation is not a matter of gratified desire but of faithful duty. He engages in battle, therefore, only because he has been appointed, not because he wants recognition. Aragorn thus urges Éowyn to find honor in doing deeds that may finally go unhonored. He calls her to act on the virtue that has no external reward but that possesses its own intrinsic merit. The ancient pagans were not alone in exalting salutary acts that win no worldly renown. "What does it profit a man," asks Jesus in a similar fashion, "to gain the whole world and forfeit his life?" (Mark 8:36). Yet it is not only to deeds of inherent worth that Jesus summons his followers, but rather to cross-bearing discipleship—to a virtue that finds its goal in a Kingdom at once in the world and yet beyond the world.

Far subtler and more deceptive is the imprudence implicit in Éowyn's romantic love for Aragorn. She is drawn to him because he is a lordly figure, a man of valorous deeds. She tries to win his affection by addressing him in the most intimate terms. Gradually she resorts to the affectionate "thee" rather than the polite "you." When Aragorn reminds her that she has no command to march southward, there to encounter the forces of Sauron, she replies in seductive terms: "Neither have those others who go with thee. They go only because they would not be parted from thee— because they love thee" (3.58). Aragorn is pained at being unable to requite Éowyn's love, yet he could not possibly return it. He is already betrothed to the elven maiden Arwen. As a man of unbreakable integrity, Aragorn cannot even entertain the possibility of loving another. More importantly, he sees that Éowyn's love is romantic in the bad sense: it's an infatuation. She has no experience of Aragorn that would enable her truly to know and love him. She is enamored, instead, with his image. She seeks her own exaltation by partaking of his gallant persona. Hence Aragorn's prudential wisdom in making this confession to her brother Éomer:

> Few other griefs amid the ill chances of this world have more bitterness and shame for a man's heart than to behold the love of a lady so fair and brave that cannot be returned. . . . And yet, Éomer, I say to you that she loves you more truly than me; for you she loves and knows; but in me she loves only a shadow and a thought: a hope of glory and great deeds, and lands far from the fields of Rohan. (3.143)

When Éowyn finally finds her marital match in Faramir, son of Denethor the steward of Gondor, they are not only united by romantic attraction but also by common experience. They have both been injured in the battle of Pelennor Fields—where Éowyn acquitted herself valiantly indeed. In the Houses of Healing they come to know each other as wounded warriors rather than exalted heroes. They back rather than run into love. Faramir discerns that Éowyn's beauty is linked with her suffering—"that her loveliness amid her grief would pierce his heart" (3.237). She in turn gradually softens her stern will as she learns to wait patiently with Faramir for the return of Aragorn and his armies.

Romantic love is less a matter of intention, Tolkien suggests, than of inadvertence. Not for nothing are we said to *fall* in love. Passion rightly implies something that we undergo rather than undertake. Tolkien knows that *eros* in the classic sense does not mean genital arousal but a longing that summons us out of ourselves, a desire for an object radically other than ourselves, a yearning that itself brings satisfaction greater than any grossly satisfied appetite. Perhaps the most classically erotic moment in the entire 1,200-page epic occurs when Faramir and Éowyn are walking along the fortress walls. They find their hands meeting and clasping, "though they did not know it. And still they waited for they knew not what" (3.240). They await an undetermined future because they have been wafted out of all selfish interest into a true and lasting regard for each other. They have learned the wisdom of love.

Prudence, Wisdom, and Moral Growth

Prudence is also closely linked with a willingness to receive counsel from others—especially from wise friends such as Gandalf. Repeatedly the Fellowship is made to recognize its utter dependence on Gandalf's superior knowledge and prudential wisdom. When Gandalf learns that Bilbo has lied about his acquisition of the Ring, he is determined to discover what actually happened. What seems to be a throwaway line nonetheless strikes with real force: "the wizard seemed to think the truth important" (1.22). Truth is important because it is not transient but perduring: the one sure guide to life. Though the novel's action has an ancient pre-Christian setting, readers can hardly fail to note the immense currency—in a world where nothing seems stable, everything out of joint, the times vexed beyond belief—of Tolkien's insistence on the sheer objectivity of truth and goodness and beauty. It comes to its clearest expression in this exchange between Éomer and Aragorn:

> "The world is all grown strange," [declared Éomer]. "Elf and Dwarf in company walk in our daily fields; and folk speak with the Lady of the Wood and yet live; and the Sword comes back to war that was broken in the long ages ere the fathers of our

fathers rode into the Mark! How shall a man judge what to do in such times?"

"As he ever has judged," said Aragorn. "Good and ill have not changed since yesteryear; nor are they one thing among Elves and Dwarves and another among Men. It is a man's part to discern them, as much in the Golden Wood as in his own house." (2.40–41)

Without the wise truthfulness of Aragorn and Gandalf and Treebeard, the Quest would never have succeeded. Yet Gandalf is noted for the dark candor of his counsel. Like the Hebrew prophets, he rarely if ever recommends a convenient or easy course of action. After long absences in search of the truth about the situation the Company actually faces, he often returns with "tidings of grief and danger." "Gandalf Stormcrow" is the derisive name that Gríma Wormtongue gives Gandalf because of his ominous prophecies. His searing truthfulness angers and disappoints those who want cheering news and easy direction. Yet it cannot be otherwise, Gandalf explains, since he is called to discern and report the truth. He is no avuncular figure giving unasked advice, as he himself confesses: "I come seldom but when my help is needed" (3.21).

Prudence is often allied with magnanimity—with a generosity and openness that abjures all small-souled greed and self-interest. Above all the other virtues, prudence enables moral growth, for prudent persons become increasingly able to act in ways that are appropriate to their circumstances. They conform themselves to the transcendent moral reality that always commands their obedience. The Lord of the Rings is a book with enduring appeal because nearly every member of the Company undergoes immense moral and spiritual growth. Unlike there-and-back-again adventures, which enable one to return home not greatly changed, the Quest leaves everyone allied with the Company profoundly altered for the good. Even Boromir, the single betrayer of the Company's cause, dies well.

Prudence is not limited to the intellectually brilliant and the learned. It often characterizes those who lack formal education and worldly shrewdness, but whose uncomplicated minds and wills are conformed to the life of virtue. Hence the psalmist's declaration that "the testimony of the LORD is sure, making wise the simple" (19:7).

Merry and Pippin, the youngest and most inexperienced of the hobbits, are turned into moral adults by means of their year-long Quest. Thus do they astonish their old friends, who can hardly recognize them when they return to the Shire—and not only because the Entdraughts have made them grow so rapidly. Their heightened physical stature is also a sign of their surprising spiritual growth. So do Legolas and Gimli experience immense moral enhancement. They begin as historic enemies but end as reconciled friends; in fact, Gimli joins Legolas on his final voyage to Valinor.

Though he is the best of the hobbits from the start, Frodo's moral enhancement is revealed in his boundless mercy, his unswerving sense of what is right, his unbending devotion to the destruction of the Ring, even if Sauron defeats him in the end. Yet surely it is the bumbling Samwise Gamgee who experiences the largest moral growth. He begins as the unquestioning servant and naïve tagalong, eager to see elves and "oliphaunts." With his peasant grammar and manners and imagination, Sam is an unlikely candidate for heroism. Yet he ends as the thoughtful and valiant bearer of Frodo up the steep slopes of Mount Doom, and finally he returns home as the future mayor of Hobbiton. He also restores the natural world of the Shire after it had been ravaged by Saruman's servants.

Gandalf can set sail for the Grey Havens at the end because he is assured that the Company has achieved the moral and spiritual wisdom that will sustain them throughout the remainder of their lives. They have undergone a tremendous sanctification—to use the standard Christian term. Tolkien himself described the moral structure of his work as "primarily . . . the ennoblement (or sanctification) of the humble" (L, 237). His characters acquire both dignity and sanctity in their faithfulness to each other, to the Quest, even to Ilúvatar himself. Like Virgil blessing Dante at the close of the *Purgatorio*, Gandalf crowns and miters his friends as true lords over themselves. He also echoes Jesus' own departure from his disciples in the Fourth Gospel, albeit with a notable difference: Jesus leaves in order that he might send the Counselor to "guide you into all the truth" (John 16:13). The Holy Spirit will accompany Christ's followers along the hard path of faith, until he meets them again at the final resurrection. Despite huge disparities in the two farewells, the similarities must also be marked. Gandalf can leave his companions behind because the rigors and temptations they have suffered, the acts of sacrifice and solidarity they have performed, will enable them to live virtuously without his aid:

> "I am with you at present," said Gandalf, "but soon I shall not be. I am not coming to the Shire. You must settle its affairs yourselves; that is what you have been trained for. Do you not yet understand? My time is over: it is no longer my task to set things to rights, nor to help folk to do so. And as for you, my dear friends, you will need no help. You are grown up now. Grown indeed very high; among the great you are, and I have no longer any fear at all for any of you." (3.275)

Gandalf is the perfect embodiment of wisdom and prudence from the book's opening to its close. Only rarely do we find him making any errors in judgment—when he trusts Saruman at Isengard and when he leaves Gollum's trail. Yet he too experiences enormous moral transformation, even a virtual apotheosis—from Gandalf the Grey to Gandalf the White. His deepest wisdom is displayed most impressively in his surprising stratagem for overcoming the Ring's power—namely, by sending it back to the Cracks of Doom and destroying it in the fires whence it was first forged. Erestor the Elflord calls Gandalf's policy both foolish and despairing, perhaps hoping that the Company might simply abandon the Ring and thus be unbothered by Sauron. Erestor lacks not only the prudential insight to discern moral subtlety; he also fails to see that Gandalf has access to a wisdom that radically transcends simplistic prudence:

> "Despair, or folly?" said Gandalf. "It is not despair, for despair is only for those who see the end beyond all doubt. We do not. It is wisdom to recognize necessity, when all other courses have been weighed, though as folly it may appear to those who cling to false hope. Well, let folly be our cloak, a veil before the eyes of the Enemy! For he is very wise, and weighs all things to a nicety in the scales of his malice. But the only measure he knows is desire, desire for power; and so he judges all hearts. Into his heart the thought will not enter that any will refuse it, that having the Ring we may seek to destroy it. If we seek this, we shall put him out of reckoning." (1.282–83)

The Limits of Prudence and the "Folly" of Self-Surrendering Sacrifice

One must virtually stop one's ears to keep from hearing echoes of the very similar summons that St. Paul makes to the Christians at Corinth. Paul repeatedly reminds them that the unbelieving world regards the gospel of salvation by suffering as mere foolishness: "For the word of the cross is folly to those who are perishing, but to us who are being saved it is the power of God. . . . Has not God made foolish the wisdom of the world? . . . For the foolishness of God is wiser than men, and the weakness of God is stronger than men. . . . God chose what is foolish in the world to shame the wise" (1 Cor. 1:18, 20, 25, 27).

Sauron possesses the wisdom of this world, since he is a minion of the one who serves as its prince and ruler (John 12:31). He believes that anyone holding the Ring of power will use it to obtain even greater power. In the fallen world, the rich want more riches, the strong greater strength, the famous still larger fame. Such is the broken reason that prudential wisdom—whether classical or Christian—always scandalizes. "God chose what is weak in the world," Paul continues, "to shame the strong, God chose what is low and despised in the world, even things that are not [the non-entities], to bring to nothing things that are [the great and powerful]" (1 Cor. 1:27–28). This staggering piece of paradoxical wisdom—that the weak and the simple and the humble can accomplish what the mighty and the clever and the proud cannot—is also articulated by Elrond: "The road must be trod, but it will be very hard. And neither strength nor wisdom will carry us far upon it. . . . Yet such is oft the course of deeds that move the wheels of the world: small hands do them because they must, while the eyes of the great are elsewhere" (1.283).

Justice: The Virtue That Requires Mercy

The words "just" and "justice" appear in Scripture far more frequently than do references to any of the other virtues, including love. God's justice is his righteousness, his law, his commandment. It is also the divine verdict that produces either reward or punishment.

> The Spirit of the Lord GOD is upon me, because the LORD has anointed me to bring good tidings to the afflicted; he has sent me to bind up the brokenhearted, to proclaim liberty to the captives, and the opening of the prison to those who are bound; to proclaim the year of the LORD's favor, and the day of vengeance of our God; to comfort all who mourn.... For I the LORD love justice, I hate robbery and wrong; I will faithfully give them their recompense, and I will make an everlasting covenant with them. . . . For as the earth brings forth its shoots, and as a garden causes what is sown in it to spring up, so the Lord GOD will cause righteousness and praise to spring forth before all the nations. (Isa. 61:1–2, 8, 11)

Justice in the biblical sense is closely related to what is called "doom" in both *The Lord of the Rings* and Christian tradition: at Doomsday justice shall finally be realized. God's people are called to live justly, in the confidence that God not only *commands* justice, but also that he himself *is* the utterly just Lord. He alone can discriminate between the righteous and the wicked; he alone ensures that all people, whether here or hereafter, receive what is due to them; he alone can grant true mercy. The Jewish prophets are vehement, moreover, in their denunciation of Israel's kings and rulers who fail to maintain policies that secure justice, especially for widows and orphans, for the poor and "the needy of the land." Jesus is no less relentless in his cry for justice, especially in his denunciation of the injustices committed by those who are religious: "Woe to you, scribes and Pharisees, hypocrites! for you tithe mint and dill and cummin, and have neglected the weightier matters of the law, justice and mercy and faith; these you ought to have done, without neglecting the others. You blind guides, straining out a gnat and swallowing a camel!" (Matt. 23:23–24).

Justice has a similarly high status in the pagan world, certainly in the world of ancient Greece and Rome that Tolkien admired no less than he honored the Scandinavian and Germanic realms. If prudence discerns the good, justice enacts it. The good man is the just man, the one who renders others their due, especially when a debt is owed. Every sin, it follows, is an injustice; for sin is the refusal to seek the good of the other, the good of the community, and thus the good that God himself wills. As in classical teaching, so in the Bible is justice considered the key to social existence: "If your brother becomes poor, and cannot maintain himself with you, you shall maintain him; as a stranger and sojourner he shall live with you. Take no interest from him or increase, but fear your God; that your brother may live beside you" (Lev. 25:35–36).

Justice requires that we grant not only our own kind what is rightly theirs, but also that we provide strangers and aliens their just recompense. To deprive them of what they are due is also to harm ourselves, for we thereby cut ourselves off from those who are vital to our own existence. We cannot be fully ourselves except through just relations with others—*all* others. In every thought and word and deed, it follows, we are either adding to or subtracting from the world's justice. Every human act turns us into either creditors or debtors—as we either restore or rob others of what justly belongs to them. The hobbit penchant for party-giving acknowledges this fundamental fact—as they find it more blessed to give than to get. The hobbits, we thus learn, "were hospitable and delighted in parties, and in presents, which they gave away freely and eagerly accepted" (1.11).

They seem to understand that nothing that we own is strictly ours. All our possessions belong to the treasury of gifts that God has given to everyone. To show hospitality to others, especially strangers, is to manifest this fundamental human commonality. Hospitality is central to both the religion of the Bible and the customs of most ancient cultures, where strangers are made guests. Scripture is replete with commands to welcome aliens: "When a stranger sojourns with you in your land, you shall not do him wrong. The stranger who sojourns with you shall be to you as the native among you, and you shall love him as yourself; for you were strangers in the land of Egypt" (Lev. 19:33–34). Jesus repeatedly relies on the hospitality of others, and he commends it, in Matthew 25, as a key distinction between those who have served him and those who have not. Jesus also insists that hospitality be shown to those who cannot reciprocate: "When you give a dinner or banquet, do not invite your friends or your brothers or your kinsmen or rich neighbors, lest they also invite you in return, and you be repaid. But when you give a feast, invite the poor, the maimed, the lame, the blind, and you will be blessed, because they cannot repay you" (Luke 14:12–14).

A gracious welcome for weary travelers is so vital to the ethos of Middle-earth that, when diminished or omitted, it gives cause for special notice—as Gandalf sharply reminds the king of Rohan: "The courtesy of your hall is somewhat lessened of late, Théoden son of Thengel" (2.118). Yet this one occasion is an exception to the rule. Throughout *The Lord of the Rings,* the Fellowship repeatedly benefits from the hospitality shown to them along their way—from Farmer Cotton at the very beginning, through the various good offices of Tom Bombadil, Elrond, Galadriel, Faramir, the Riders of Rohan; on to Treebeard's generous hosting of Merry and Pippin toward the end. Aragorn performs a veritably epic act of hospitality when he opens up the entire realm of Gondor for the celebration of his marriage to Arwen. Hospitality thus proves crucial to the practice of justice in Middle-earth, since the free giving and receiving of gifts ensures that no one seeks merely his own good.

The Complacency of the Safe and the Satisfied

After having my students describe the various qualities of life in the Shire—whose quaint practices and idiosyncratic habits are at once amusing and endearing—I often ask them to name the hobbits' chief problem. A long pause usually follows. The students' silence is quite revealing. The hobbits' problem is, ironically, that they have no problems. They enjoy a virtually Edenic existence—so peaceful are their relations, so delightful are their pleasures, so just are their laws. The life of the Shire constitutes, in fact, Tolkien's vision of life as it is supposed to be lived. Hobbits were not meant to bear the burdens of the world, but rather to preserve a last unspoiled corner of Middle-earth as a haven of modest and exemplary life. Yet the hobbits have lived in safety and comfort for so long that they are threatened by complacency and self-satisfaction. Since they have had no emergencies in recent memory, they assume that crises will never arise. Inward complacency and decay, Tolkien suggests, is altogether as threatening as outward assault. Thus have the hobbits come to take for granted what should have been a perennial cause for both vigilance and thanksgiving—the protection provided them by many unknown friends outside the Shire:

> There in that pleasant corner of the world they plied their well-ordered business of living, and they heeded less and less the world outside where dark things moved, until they came to think that peace and plenty were the rule in Middle-earth and the right of all sensible folk. They forgot or ignored what little they had ever known of the Guardians, and of the labours of those that made possible the long peace of the Shire. They were, in fact, sheltered, but they had ceased to remember it. (1.14)

The hobbits are far from ruined by their life of ease. Quite to the contrary, they are "still curiously tough" (1.15)—able, if pressed, to do without the good things that they rightly delight in. Even so, Tolkien does not exempt the hobbits from the temptations that beset all other creatures. When Gandalf informs Frodo that he has been called to destroy the Ring, the hobbit protests that he is "not made for perilous quests." He asks the wizard why he rather than someone else has been elected to undertake so impossible a mission. Gandalf knows that Frodo is the noblest of hobbits, yet the wizard assures him that a very deep mystery lurks in his vocation concerning the Ring, even as he warns Frodo never to presume on his own incorruptibility: "'Such questions [about chosenness] cannot be answered,' said Gandalf. 'You may be sure that it was not for any merit that others do not possess: not for power or wisdom at any rate. But you have been chosen, and you must therefore use such strength and heart and wits as you have'" (1.70).

Though the Shire is immediately threatened by the lurking presence of Saruman's and Sauron's agents, the perennial temptation of the hobbits arises from their own fallen nature. The Company's commitment to justice requires them to combat their own injustice—especially the anti-communal sin of greed. Like Dante before him, Tolkien singles out the one evil that besets all creatures—whether hobbits or men, whether elves or dwarves, whether wizards or even valar: the injustice of *cupiditas*, greed.

Here again Tolkien takes his stand with the biblical insistence that "the love of money is the root of all evils; it is through this craving that some have wandered away from the faith and pierced their hearts with many pangs" (1 Tim. 6:10). Greed is the primal form of injustice, for it seeks one's own good at the expense of others. Chaucer's Pardoner affirms this danger in a well-worn maxim: *Radix malorum est cupiditas*. The root of evil lies in greed and thus in a lust for money, money that will satisfy our desire for possessions, possessions that are meant to cushion us against discomfort and disaster. Such are the links in the chain of *cupiditas* that binds nearly everyone. It has turned Gollum, as we have seen, into a twisted and pathetic caricature of himself.

Greed also holds Bilbo at least briefly in thrall. Though he found the Ring by the "luck" that we gradually discover to have been providential, Bilbo falsifies the nature of his discovery. He claims that Gollum promised to give it to him as a "present" for winning the riddle contest, and that he thus owns the ring by right rather than chance. Truth is the first casualty not only of war, Tolkien shows, but also of greed. Saruman is so greedy for the power of the Ring that his mind and will have been bent totally out of shape by it. He is unable to accept the freedom of Gandalf's pardon—which will be given if only Saruman will surrender his staff and the key to his fortress-tower of Orthanc, after his armies have been defeated at the battle of Helm's Deep. Consumed by his selfishness, Saruman is infuriated by the merciful Gandalf's promise to return his two tokens of good conduct at some later time:

> Saruman's face grew livid, twisted with rage, and a red light kindled in his eyes. He laughed wildly. "Later!" he cried, and his voice rose to a scream. "Later! Yes, when you also have the Keys of Barad-dûr itself, I suppose; and the crowns of seven kings, and the rods of the Five Wizards, and have purchased yourself a pair of boots many sizes larger than those that you wear now. A modest plan. Hardly one in which my help is needed! I have other things to do. Do not be a fool. If you wish to treat with me, while you have a chance, go away, and come back when you are sober! And leave behind these cut-throats and small rag-tag that dangle at your tail!" (2.188)

This is Tolkien's frightful picture of maniacal intransigence, utter self-delusion, pathetic rage—as maddened greed prefers misery to mercy. Saruman the once-revered wizard has reduced himself to casting stupid insults at Gandalf's companions and hobbit friends.

The fundamental urge to possessiveness is most repugnantly displayed in the giant all-devouring spider Shelob. She is allied with neither Sauron nor Saruman: she is consumed by a rapacity that is entirely her own—as she feeds vampirishly on the blood of living creatures. Shelob uses her gross obesity not only to capture but also to kill her prey, squashing them to death. It is not surprising that she should find a companion in Gollum, for he is snared in the same sin, albeit for different reasons. Tolkien depicts Shelob as especially disgusting, perhaps in order to signal the moral as well as the physical flabbiness of our own culture of consumption:

> She served none but herself, drinking the blood of Elves and Men, bloated and grown fat with endless brooding on her feasts, weaving webs of shadow; for all living things were her food, and her vomit darkness. Far and wide her lesser broods, bastards of the miserable mates, her own offspring, that she slew, spread from glen to glen. . . . But her lust was not [Gollum's] lust. Little she knew of or cared for towers, or rings, or anything devised by mind or hand, who only desired death for all others, mind and body, and for herself a glut of life, alone, swollen till the mountains could no longer hold her up and the darkness could not contain her. (2.332–33)

The Necessity and Limits of War

Tolkien acknowledges the hard fact that evil assaults the Company not only from within but also from without. While such inner allurements as greed work by way of seduction, the coercions of Sauron are primarily external. In the end, as we have seen, Frodo is overwhelmed by the despotic magnetism of the Ring. These two sorts of sin cannot be combated, however, in the same fashion. Internal evils are to be resisted by spiritual and moral discipline, but external injustices must be halted with force. Not to employ all the might of the Free Peoples in the fight against Sauron is to consent to his evil. Worse still, it is to leave defenseless the "little people" who are ground to bits by the tyrannous forces of history. Tolkien is no pacifist.

Perhaps because the heroic cultures of the ancient North were centered on the prowess of warriors, Tolkien repeatedly hails the valor of soldiers, whether ancient or modern, who are willing to die in defense of their country and people. "Let us by all means esteem the old heroes," Tolkien writes, "men caught in the chains of circumstance or of their own character, torn between duties equally sacred, dying with their backs to the wall" (MC, 17). "The wages of heroism is death," Tolkien also observed, in deliberate alteration of St. Paul's saying in Romans 6:23 concerning the wages of sin. It seems clear that Tolkien wants to demonstrate what is immensely admirable, especially in our spiritually inert age, about this ancient "exaltation of undefeated will, . . . this indomitability, this paradox of defeat inevitable yet unacknowledged." The heroism of our antique forbears is still relevant for our time, Tolkien insists, because it reveals the most fundamental human struggle: "man at war with the hostile world, and his inevitable overthrow in Time" (MC, 18).

The Lord of the Rings remains a remarkably unpagan book for disclosing what is dangerous in traditional heroism. Tolkien observes, in fact, that "malice, greed, destruction [are] the evil side of heroic life" (MC, 17). No pagan delight in killing one's own kind is present anywhere in Tolkien's work. Since every creature of Ilúvatar is essentially good until inveigled by evil, Tolkien has his heroes repeatedly extend mercy to defeated enemies. Yet there is no forgiveness for the minions of Sauron. The orcs and Uruk-hai are wholly evil, and to slay them is to experience the joy of justice. At the battle of Pelennor Fields, Éomer fights as "the lord of a fell people," a fierce warrior who has the "lust of battle" on him (3.122). Even the generous King Théoden, having been aroused from the defeatist spell that Gríma had cast upon him, leads his army in self-abandoned fury, as they find delight in slaughtering hellions:

Fey he seemed, or the battle-fury of his fathers ran like new fire in his veins, and he was born up on Snowmane [his horse] like a god of old. . . . . His golden shield was uncovered, and lo! it shone like an image of the Sun, and the grass flamed into green about the white feet of his steed. . . . [A]ll the host of Rohan burst into song, and they sang as they slew, for the joy of battle was on them, and the sound of their singing that was fair and terrible came even to the City. (3.112–13)

Tolkien the Christian knows that to combat evil by justified force requires a right understanding of war, lest it produce new and worse evils. Over against the rapturous killing that usually results even from wars fought in defense of the good, we encounter the drastically chastened estimate of war provided by Faramir. He is no coward skulking in fear of death. On the contrary, Faramir is the brother of brave Boromir, and like him he is gladly willing to die fighting evil while defending the good. But whereas Boromir became proud and rash in his fearlessness, Faramir offers a modest vision of warfare. He articulates a pre-Christian version of what has become known as the "just war" vindication of combat under radically restrained conditions. Faramir takes no pleasure in the splendor and grandeur of war. He sanctions it only for defensive, non-retaliatory purposes, and in behalf of the freedom and civility that war may sometimes secure:

"For myself," said Faramir, "I would see the White Tree [which once grew in the citadel of Gondor as its chief emblem] in flower again in the courts of the kings, and the Silver Crown return, and Minas Tirith in peace: Minas Anor again as of old, full of light, high and fair, beautiful as a queen among other queens: not a mistress of many slaves, nay, not even a kind mistress of willing slaves. War must be, while we defend our lives against a destroyer who would devour all; but I do not love the bright sword for its sharpness, nor the arrow for its swiftness, nor the warrior for his glory. I love only that which they defend: the city of the Men of Númenor; and I would have her loved for her memory, her ancientry, her beauty, and her present wisdom. Nor feared, save as men may fear the dignity of a man, old and wise." (2.280)

No such speech could ever be found in a book from the heroic cultures that Tolkien so greatly admired. Even more anomalous is the attitude toward killing that Frodo espouses at the end of *The Lord of the Rings*. Perhaps because he has himself been permanently scarred by the violence of compulsive evil, Frodo orders a quasi-pacifist scouring of the Shire. In his year-long absence, Hobbiton has been taken over by the henchmen of Saruman, who have imposed a reign of terror and suspicion on the region. The Shire must be cleansed of these ruffians if peace and liberty are to be restored. Yet Frodo refuses to allow any "slaying of hobbits, not even if they have gone over to the other side. . . . No hobbit" he points out, "has ever killed another on purpose in the Shire, and it is not to begin now. And nobody is to be killed at all, if it can be helped. Keep your tempers and hold your hands to the last possible moment!" (3.285). The best of all hobbits himself refuses to participate in killing of any kind: "Frodo had been in the battle, but he had not drawn sword, and his chief part had been to prevent the hobbits in their wrath at their losses, from slaying those of their enemies who threw down their weapons" (3.295–96). Again, these are remarkable claims to come from a novel with a pagan and heroic setting, for they demonstrate the evils that can be committed while resisting injustice.

The Blindness of Justice and the Call to Mercy and Deference

Christian tradition overcomes the limits of human justice by insisting that it can never be divorced from divine mercy. To hold the scales of equity in her hands while blindfolded, as the goddess of Justice usually does, is to run the risk of misconstruing the relation between mercy and justice. The problem is indeed acute. Since justice insists that all people get their due, and since mercy implies that at least some receive what is not their due, how can the two claims avoid contradiction? The answer lies in the biblical understanding of our relation to God. He does not owe us our existence but grants it as sheer miraculous gift. There is nothing we could possibly do to compensate for this gift, to make it something deserved—not even to return it. We would be totally indebted even if we were unfallen. Sin hugely magnifies our obligation to the triune God. His deliverance of us from bondage through Israel and

Christ and the church makes the debt absolute. In the deepest sense, therefore, God's mercy precedes his justice and serves as its very basis. His judgment is but the enforcement of his mercy: God insists that we live by the same merciful measure wherein we have been created and redeemed.

Tolkien repeatedly demonstrates his understanding of this profound paradox that mercy is not contrary to justice but the true realization of it. Over and again we encounter characters who have done wrong and who deserve punishment, but who receive justice in the form of mercy—as their bad deeds often issue in surprisingly good things. Although Éowyn broke her orders to remain behind in order to become the steward of Rohan, her disobedience helped win the battle of Pelennor Fields—as she first slew the fell beast that carried the Witch-king and then killed the dreadful Lord of the Nazgûl himself. King Théoden had also ordered Merry to stay behind. Yet in his refusal to avoid the fray, Merry not only prevents the Witch-king from slaying Éowyn, but also joins her in actually massacring the monster. Had either of them acted on or been recompensed according to the strict rules of justice, the struggle would surely have been lost.

Another example of the mercy that transcends justice is to be found in Pippin's laudable curiosity. He is driven by a desire to know. Yet his inquisitiveness causes him to become obsessed with the *palantír* after Gríma hurls it down from Orthanc. Even though Sauron had used the seeing stone to manipulate Saruman, Pippin becomes fascinated with its power, and thus steals it from the sleeping Gandalf. By looking into it, Pippin experiences the horror of revealing his whereabouts to Sauron. Rather than reprimand the overly curious hobbit, however, Gandalf treats him mercifully, pointing out how narrowly Pippin escaped the deadly vengeance of Sauron that his curiosity could have unleashed:

> You have taken no harm. There is no lie in your eyes, as I feared. But [Sauron] did not speak long with you. A fool, but an honest fool, you remain, Peregrin Took. Wiser ones might have done worse in such a pass. But mark this! You have been saved, and all your friends too, mainly by good fortune, as it is called. You cannot count on it a second time. (2.199)

The gift of deliverance—whether by means of luck or providence—is not to be abused. As Paul might have warned Pippin, we are not to sin in order that grace might abound (Rom. 6:1).

Those who exercise justice err not only when they fail to render mercy unto others, but also—and even more egregiously—when they boast of their own justice. We have heard Boromir prating about his pure desire to use the Ring in combat against Sauron. His moral arrogance was surely a major cause of his downfall. Scripture always depicts such false righteousness as the worst of all evils: it ignores human fallibility, and it denies the mercy of God as our one guard against it. Paul inveighs against those who boast of their own obedience to the law, when in fact everyone depends equally on the mercy that enables true righteousness: "For there is no distinction; since all have sinned and fall short of the glory of God, they are justified by his grace as a gift through the redemption which is in Christ Jesus" (Rom. 3:22–24). So does Jesus utter sharp words against those who would take pride in their obedience to the law: "when you have done all that is commanded of you, say, 'We are unworthy servants; we have only done what was our duty'" (Luke 17:10).

Worship and prayer are the appointed Christian means for avoiding all blustering self-righteousness: they honor the incarnate and living God for his incomparable gifts. These acts of obeisance and petition demonstrate that we could not possibly recompense God's mercies. They also show that, in being utterly grateful, we have no vain desire to reimburse God. Though Tolkien does not have the hobbits either worship or pray, he revives a third and much-neglected means of honoring those to whom we owe an unpayable debt: *courteous deference*. Sam Gamgee knows that Frodo Baggins is truly his superior—and not only because Sam comes from peasant stock, as his poor grammar, his fear of things foreign, and his social ineptitude all indicate. Far more profoundly, Sam defers to Frodo because he comprehends Frodo's moral excellence. For all these reasons, therefore, Sam always addresses him as "Mr. Frodo." He recognizes, without fail, who is master and who is servant. Far from demeaning him, Sam's attitude of courteous deference lifts him to his own distinctive excellence. He becomes, in fact, the book's real hero.

So does Pippin, the youngest and smallest of the hobbits, find himself strangely exalted by swearing loyalty to Denethor, the unstable and untrustworthy steward of Gondor. Pippin knows that he is not natively inclined to valor; on the contrary, he confesses his own fear of warfare. Yet he also knows that Boromir, Denethor's faulty son, had died courageously and sacrificially while fighting the orcs, thus saving him and Merry from sure capture. Thus does Pippin offer his service to the deceptive old Denethor in a ceremony that echoes the marriage service in the *Book of Common Prayer*:

> Here do I swear fealty and service to Gondor, and to the Lord and Steward of the realm, to speak and to be silent, to do and to let be, to come and to go, in need or plenty, in peace or war, in living or dying, from this hour henceforth, until my lord release me, or death take me, or the world end. So say I, Peregrin son of Paladin of the Shire of the Halflings. (3.28)

To be "courteous" is to comport oneself as if one were in the court of a king or a queen. The language of courtesy is elevated because it calls for elevated conduct. Knowing that Pippin is being summoned to act in a magnanimous way, Gandalf refuses to chide him for his heartfelt if also dangerous act: "generous deed should not be checked by cold counsel" (3.32). Pippin finds, in fact, that his deferential gesture has lifted him to a superior plane of respect: "he could not be rid of his new rank, only fitting, men thought, to one befriended by Boromir and honoured by the Lord Denethor; and they thanked him for coming among them, and hung on his words and stories of the outlands, and gave him as much food and ale as he could wish" (3.40). The once-frightened hobbit acquits himself exceedingly well at the Black Gate of Mordor, slaying the terrible troll-chief even as he is himself almost killed. As he loses consciousness, Pippin retains the amused insouciance that enabled his original act of deference: "'So it ends as I guessed it would,' his thought said, even as it fluttered away; and it laughed a little within him ere it fled, almost gay it seemed to be casting off all doubt and care and fear" (3.169).

Courage: The Virtue That Issues in Endurance

If prudence and justice are virtues of the mind and spirit, courage and temperance are virtues having to do with the body. Fortitude is an approach to life that is explicitly linked with death. "Courage," said G. K. Chesterton, "is almost a contradiction in terms. It means a strong desire to live taking the form of a readiness to die." In the pagan realm, courage is supremely manifested when one dies in battle while defending a just cause. In the Christian world, it is a willingness to die as a martyr rather than denying Christ, or else to refuse to kill others only in order to preserve one's own life. Even when courage does not require the shedding of our blood, it always entails a refusal to love our lives so much that we lose our souls. Courage refuses to commit sin because of fear. It makes war against the brute power of evil with all the strength of one's body and soul. As its name indicates, courage is located at the center of our being, in the *cor*—the heart and its intentions. We are called to courage in order to preserve our integrity before others and in the presence of God: to keep ourselves morally and spiritually intact.

Scripture is rife with calls to courage, whether in escaping Egyptian bondage or in conquering the Promised Land. Many of the Old Testament heroes are warriors such as Gideon. There is also the venerable biblical tradition of righteous wrath and good ire—the anger that despises the things that God despises. "Do I not hate them that hate thee, O LORD?" cries the psalmist (139:21). While the New Testament has no soldier saints, Jesus is no milquetoast Lord. He acts with considerable vehemence in cleansing the temple of the money changers and other commercializers. At the same time, he strictly forbids his disciples to take up arms and fight. On the contrary, Christ enjoins his followers to turn the other cheek, to walk the second mile, to make friends with accusers, even to pray for enemies. The life of spiritual courage rather than martial bravery finds its most eloquent and profound expression in Paul's exhortation to the church at Corinth:

> We put no obstacle in any one's way, so that no fault may be found with our ministry, but as servants of God we commend

ourselves in every way: through great endurance, in afflictions, hardships, calamities, beatings, imprisonments, tumults, labors, watching, hunger; by purity, knowledge, forbearance, kindness, the Holy Spirit, genuine love, truthful speech, and the power of God; with the weapons of righteousness for the right hand and for the left; in honor and dishonor, in ill repute and good repute. We are treated as impostors, and yet are true; as unknown, and yet well known; as dying, and behold we live; as punished, and yet not killed; as sorrowful, yet always rejoicing; as poor, yet making many rich; as having nothing, and yet possessing everything. (2 Cor. 6:3–10)

Heroic and Supernal Courage

The Lord of the Rings is filled with so many instances of heroic courage, some quite grim, that it is not necessary to catalogue them. Suffice it to mention that Legolas and Gimli keep count of the orcs they have killed, as if they were engaged in a contest. Aragorn climbs the walls of Helm's Deep and stands defiantly alone against the orcs, ordering them to be gone. At the same battle, the elderly King Théoden mounts a final desperate charge, not letting death come to him in sickness and old age, but fighting Saruman's forces until they kill him. Much less obvious than such instances of traditional heroism is another kind of sacrifice that the Company makes: the willingness to lay down their lives without real hope of victory, especially at the end when there seems to be no chance of defeating Sauron. Before the final battle at the Black Gate of Mordor, Gandalf calls for an unprudential kind of courage. "Prudence," he points out, "would counsel you to strengthen such strong places as you have, and there await the onset. . . . I do not counsel prudence," he adds. "I said victory could not be achieved by arms. I still hope for victory, but not by arms" (3.154–55).

Rather does Gandalf summon the Company to a supernal kind of surrender, a giving up of power in order to defeat Power. Hoping that Sam and Frodo may have entered Mordor, and thus be making their way toward Mount Doom, Gandalf urges his friends to mount a direct assault on Sauron's fortress, Barad-dûr. He knows that the result is likely to be death and oblivion. Yet in sending his orc and troll armies to crush the armies of the Free Peoples, Sauron may fail to notice the presence of the Ring-bearer and his companion at the peak of Mount Doom:

> We must push Sauron to his last throw. We must call out his hidden strength, so that he shall empty his land. We must march out to meet him at once. We must make ourselves the bait, though his jaws should close on us. He will take that bait, in hope and in greed, for he will think that in such rashness he sees the pride of the new Ringlord. . . . We must walk open-eyed into that trap, with courage, but with small hope for ourselves. . . . But this, I deem, is our duty. And better so than to perish nonetheless—as we surely shall, if we sit here—and know as we die that no new age shall be. (3.156)

Gandalf's call for the massed forces of the Free Peoples to serve as sacrificial lambs has biblical rather than classical echoes. Luke quotes Isaiah 53 to describe Christ as "a sheep led to the slaughter" (Acts 8:32). Paul cites Psalm 44 in calling Christians to retain confidence in God in even the worst of circumstances: "For thy sake we are being killed all day long; we are regarded as sheep to be slaughtered" (Rom. 8:36). And Jesus commissions his disciples to a life that is sure to bring persecution and perhaps death: "Behold, I send you out as sheep in the midst of wolves" (Matt. 10:16).

The Danger of Fearlessness

Courage and fearlessness are not synonymous. Those who have lost the will to live and who thus have no fear of death can hardly be called courageous. "Courage," declared Mark Twain, "is resistance to fear, mastery of fear—not absence of fear." The suicidal fearlessness of Talibanic terrorists does not exemplify courage; their homicidal suicides are desperate bargains purchased in lust for glory. At the height of the Roman persecutions, the early church strictly forbade Christians from seeking their own martyrdom in the name of the Gospel. Whether among Christians or pagans, the truly courageous have neither lust for death nor scorn for life. There are many things that are rightly to be feared—

whether cancer or war, tornadoes or terrorists. Even Gandalf confesses his fear of Sauronic evil. Supremely, of course, it is the goodness and justice of God that is most greatly to be feared, for in such fear lies the real beginning of wisdom (Ps. 111:10). It is also the beginning of courage, as Josef Pieper makes clear:

> If in this supreme test, in face of which the braggart falls silent and every heroic gesture is paralyzed, a man walks straight up to the cause of his fear and is not deterred from doing that which is good; if, moreover, he does so for the sake of good—which ultimately means for the sake of God, and therefore not from ambition or from fear of being taken for a coward—this man, and he alone, is truly brave. (127)

The Lord of the Rings contains two instances of the false bravery that springs from false fearlessness. The first is found in Éowyn's heroism at the battle of Pelennor Fields. Merry discerns that she does not fight because she is convinced of the rightness of her cause and the prospect of its ultimate victory. Éowyn is literally infuriated that she has been refused her rightful role as a warrior because she is a woman. Merry notes, all too sadly, that Éowyn had "the face of one that goes seeking death, having no hope" (3.116). There is no denying the heroism of her killing the Lord of the Nazgûl, but Tolkien quietly suggests that an embittered fearlessness is no real basis either for living or dying. Éowyn will acquire true courage only when her rancor is transformed by her love for Faramir.

Sam Gamgee also learns the difference between a spurious fearlessness and true courage after he finds Frodo lying dead, as he falsely assumes, outside Shelob's Lair. He debates with himself about three different courses: to take the Ring that hangs from Frodo's neck and carry it to Mount Doom alone, to pursue and kill Gollum in grim vengeance, or to join Frodo in death by taking his own life: "He looked on the bright point of the sword. He thought of the places behind where there was a black brink and an empty fall into nothingness" (2.341). To join Frodo in self-inflicted death would seem to be a sign of courage, but it would in fact be an act of cowardice, since Sam's real calling is to carry on the Quest. Sam chooses the first of these alternatives, but then he gradually perceives that he is called to an even nobler act of solidarity in suffering alongside his master. "Certainly the Ring had grown greatly in power," Sam ruefully reflects, "as it approached the places of its forging; but one thing it did not confer, and that was courage" (2.344).

Courage in defense of one's slain lord was a high virtue in the heroic world of the ancient North. To live after one's master had died in battle was to live in shame. Yet Sam is no ancient hero. His decision to remain with the seemingly dead Frodo does not come as a deliberate choice so much as an unexpected gift. He no longer ponders his options but acts as his character dictates, recognizing that he cannot allow the orcs to desecrate Frodo's body: "He flung the Quest and all his decisions away, and fear and doubt with them. He knew now where his place was and had been: at his master's side, though what he could do there was not clear" (2.344). Though Sam fails to find Frodo immediately, he discovers from the quarreling orcs that his master is surprisingly alive, and that only in this last act of returning to Frodo's body has he exhibited authentic courage: "You fool, he isn't dead, and your heart knew it. Don't trust your head, Samwise, it is not the best part of you. The trouble with you is that you never really had any hope" (2.350).

Courage Transformed into Hopeful Endurance

The Company repeatedly exhibits the courage that springs from hope because they have been schooled in endurance. It is a courage-related virtue much prized by the ancient Stoics and fully adopted by the early Christians. Yet there is a huge gap between the two sorts of endurance. Stoics endure life both fearlessly and tearlessly, convinced that things could not be other than they are, and thus that true nobility of soul lies in taking on oneself the unfeeling character of the universe without complaint. It is the courage of the stiff upper lip and the unquivering chin. Christian endurance is another thing altogether—precisely because it is prompted by transcendent joy and hope. Only those disciples who endure "to the end," declares Jesus, "will be saved" (Matt. 24:13;

Mark 13:13). The book of Hebrews affirms that "for the joy that was set before him [Jesus] endured the cross, despising the shame" (12:2). Paul's letters are full of enjoinders for Christians to endure persecution, affliction, grief, chastenings, and the like. The Pauline passage that bears most clearly on the endurance displayed by the Fellowship is found in the letter to the Romans: "we rejoice in our sufferings, knowing that suffering produces endurance, and endurance produces character, and character produces hope, and hope does not disappoint us, because God's love has been poured into our hearts through the Holy Spirit which has been given to us" (5:3–5).

Tolkien does not violate the terms of his imaginative world by making hobbitic endurance explicitly Christian. Quite to the contrary, the hobbits' endurance sometimes seems altogether stoical. They are determined simply to slog ahead, to trudge forward no matter what, to "*see it through*," as Sam says (2.341). So does Pippin, thinking that he is about to be killed, declare simply, "I must do my best" (3.168). This phrase might well serve as the leitmotiv of Tolkien's entire epic, since it is for him the chief manifestation of the natural grace that summons every human being to moral effort. Tolkien often confessed his admiration for the noncommissioned officers who performed their duty under the horrific conditions of trench warfare during World War I. As Sam and Frodo find themselves increasingly frustrated in their attempt to ascend Mount Doom, there to cast the Ring into its fires, they seem sure to fail; yet they are nonetheless determined to struggle forward: "Still we shall have to try," said Frodo. "It's no worse than I expected. I never hoped to get across. I can't see any hope of it now. But I've still got to do the best I can" (3.201).

As they are following Gollum across the Dead Marshes toward Mordor, Frodo urges his dear companion not to vex himself with questions about what they will do when their errand is finished: "Samwise Gamgee, my dear hobbit—indeed, Sam my dearest hobbit, friend of friends—I do not think we need give thought to what comes after that. To *do the job* as you put it—what hope is there that we ever shall?" (2.231). Yet never does any member of the Company turn back. They are driven by a profound sense of duty that enables them "to do the job," to do their best, to endure to the end, even to have "hope . . . against hope" (Rom. 4:18). Like Abraham, albeit for quite different reasons, they have "patiently endured" and thus obtain the promise (Heb. 6:15).

It is appropriate to cite such biblical passages because the endurance of the Company is more often glad than grim. Though a dark sense of doom hovers over the entire epic, it is often lightened by the hobbits' recourse to poetry and song. "We seldom sing of anything more terrible than wind and rain," declares Pippin. "And most of my songs are about things that make us laugh; or about food and drink, of course" (3.80). The hobbits are most unstoical in their wonderfully self-deprecating sense of humor. Perhaps Sam is most adept at mocking himself. Searching for Frodo in Shelob's Lair, amid fearful darkness and dread, he urges himself forward with comical commands: "'Come on, you miserable sluggard!' Sam cried to himself" (3.178). Gamgee makes his way into Sauron's guard-tower of Cirith Ungol noisily rather than stealthily, as befits his clumsy rotundity. When he sets off the alarms of the orcs who have mistaken him for an elf, Sam treats the whole matter comically: "'That's done it!' said Sam. 'Now I've rung the front door bell! Well, come on somebody!' he cried. 'Tell Captain Shagrat that the great Elf-warrior has called, with his elf-sword too!'" (3.179).

Occasionally, the hobbits laugh in order to cheer themselves up—as they whistle not through the proverbial cemetery but in the real darkness of Mordor. Usually, however, hobbit laughter has deeper sources. Sometimes it springs from their delight in the wonders of the world, as when Sam and Frodo escape the Dead Marshes and enter the flowering, fragrant realm of Ithilien: "Gollum coughed and retched, but the hobbits breathed deep, and suddenly Sam laughed, for heart's ease, not for jest" (2.259). Most often the hobbits laugh because they possess the freeing capacity to stand outside themselves, to behold themselves at a critical distance, and thus not to take themselves too seriously. This freedom comes most notably to Sam in the tower of Cirith Ungol, where he thinks Frodo lies dead. Despite his despair, Sam finds himself putting his own unaccountably hopeful words to one of the "old childish tunes out of the Shire":

In western lands beneath the Sun
the flowers may rise in Spring,
the trees may bud, the waters run,
the merry finches sing.
Or there maybe 'tis cloudless night
and swaying beeches bear
the Elven-stars as jewels white
amid their branching hair.
                              (3.185)

This enduringly joyful, even comic sense of life arises from the Company's conviction that their errand constitutes a small action within a gigantic cosmic drama. Though the machinations of evil often cause them searing doubt, they believe that the victory of good is ultimately assured, even if they may themselves fail and soon be forgotten. If they are remembered at all, says Sam, it will be a jovial recollection: "'Let's hear about Frodo and the Ring!' And they'll say: 'Yes, that's one of my favourite stories. Frodo was very brave, wasn't he, dad?' 'Yes, my boy, the famousest of the hobbits, and that's saying a lot.'" "'It's saying a lot too much,' said Frodo, and he laughed a long clear laugh from his heart. Such a sound had not been heard in those places since Sauron came to Middle-earth" (2.321–22). This moment of transcendent joy occurs just prior to their entering Shelob's caves, where Sam and Frodo exhibit true courage and endurance yet again. Tolkien may have had such moments in mind when he said that, at its best, fantasy serves as "a far-off gleam or echo of *evangelium* in the real world" (MC, 155)—a distant reverberation of the Gospel.

Temperance: The Virtue That Produces Cheerful Asceticism

Like the other cardinal virtues, temperance is easily misunderstood. It is often reduced to mere moderation, an avoidance of extremes, a playing of the ends against the middle. This common-sense definition of temperance is almost always tied to excesses in eating, drinking, and having sex. Temperance deals, in fact, with these things, but never in sour self-abasement or sanctimonious scorn for the flesh. On the contrary, temperance seeks to cultivate a right regard for our bodies and souls in their inseparable integrity.

The New Testament links temperance with sobriety: "For the grace of God has appeared for the salvation of all men, training us to renounce irreligion and worldly passions, and to live sober, upright, and godly lives in this world" (Titus 2:11–12). Temperance concerns a positive discipline of precisely those activities wherein the rightful urge to preserve and perpetuate ourselves—to delight in the good pleasures of the good creation—is most insistent. Exactly because the sensuous delights of life are divinely ordained are they also exceedingly dangerous. They need to be *tempered*: to be brought to their true quality, to be given their real consistency. This may require a certain intensifying of the senses rather than their mortification—so that practitioners of temperance may have souls like tempered steel. Not to practice temperance, says St. Augustine, is to indulge in a "servile liberty."

Christian tradition vigorously denies that our bodies are the real cause of our sin. This is the Manichean heresy that Christians repudiate. Yet while the chief sins are spiritual rather than carnal, we are still called to order the life of our fleshly senses. This ordering may entail a radical asceticism, as in the case of St. Paul himself: "Every athlete exercises self-control in all things. They do it to receive a perishable wreath, but we an imperishable. Well, I do not run aimlessly, I do not box as one beating the air; but I pommel my body and subdue it, lest after preaching to others I myself should be disqualified" (1 Cor. 9:25–27). Paul's logic is clear and compelling. If athletes are willing to give up earthly pleasures for mere earthly prizes, how much more ought Christians to renounce the gratifications of physical desire for the sake of the Gospel and the Kingdom—especially since we know the Holy to be infinitely greater than even the finest human things? For Christians, in sum, temperance is the discipline that enables our full participation in the body of Christ by making Jesus the Lord of our bodies.

The earliest Christian teachings on temperance took their root from the First Epistle of John, where the world *(kosmos)* is understood as a metaphor of all that is alienated from God and has enmity toward him. From the little epistle's brief listing of three categories of sin, there gradually developed a full-fledged description and analysis of the various kinds of sins: "Do not love the world or the things that are in the world. If any one loves the world, love for the Father is not in him. For all that is in the world, the lust of the flesh and the lust of the eyes and the pride of life, is not of the Father but is of the world. And the world passes away, and the lust of it; but he who does the will of God abides for ever" (1 John 2:15–17). The three forms of concupiscence (the lust of the flesh, the lust of the eyes, and the pride of life) are not to be restrained for negative reasons alone—i.e., simply to keep them from getting out of control. Rather are they to be tempered for the sake of a certain gladness and serenity of spirit. Only in godly detachment from the world may the world's beauties and pleasures be enjoyed.

The Lust of the Flesh and the Self-Denial of Frodo and Sam

Concupiscentia is rendered all too inadequately as "lust," since our modern word connotes little other than ravenous sexual appetite and burning bodily desire. The older word suggests, far more subtly, an inordinate love of worldly things, whether they be physical or spiritual. Even when bodily cravings are satisfied wrongly, they may be reordered in ways not necessarily ascetic. The sin of gluttony, for instance, does not afflict only the overweight. In an obese culture where nearly everyone seeks to be slender—by way of constant dieting and maniacal regimens of exercise—gluttony may need to be redefined as an inordinate love of thinness. It may also need to be overcome by the cultivation of an unfastidious esteem for bodily heft. This latter-day gluttony is not a hobbitic temptation. As we have seen, the hobbits have no skepticism about the pleasures of the senses—the delights of the palate least of all. Because the hobbits are accustomed to enjoying six meals a day, Merry has but a single pressing question after the harrowing victory at Pelennor Fields: he wants to know when supper will be served!

As a deeply incarnational writer, Tolkien also understands the asceticism that is intrinsic to authentic faith. To honor the flesh is to discipline it. Jesus cannot rightly embark upon his ministry until he has recapitulated Israel's long sojourn in self-denial by way of his own wilderness encounter with demonic temptations of the flesh. Samwise Gamgee is the hobbit for whom such an ascetic life proves most difficult. More than any of his companions, he is susceptible to an intemperate desire for food. Sam is a plump fellow who relishes his victuals. Not only is he a culinary craftsman who hates to give up his cooking gear; he also grieves at the prospect of having no more well-prepared meals.

This most jovial and genial of hobbits is required, at the end, to surrender far more valuable possessions than his utensils. In their tortuous ascent up Mount Doom, he and Frodo are gradually stripped of all their comforting accoutrements. They are both humiliated by having to wear orc-gear in order to disguise themselves. Sam also gives up the elven cloak bestowed by Lady Galadriel in order that the failing Frodo might be protected by it. Eventually they abandon even their orc-gear and weapons. Yet the greater Sam's relinquishment of his creaturely devices—even as his body is wracked with hunger and thirst—the greater his moral strength: "Sam's plain hobbit-face grew stern, almost grim, as the will hardened in him, and he felt through all his limbs a thrill, as if he was turning into some creature of stone or steel that neither despair nor weariness nor endless barren miles could subdue" (3.211). When Sam is at last forced to carry the virtually helpless Frodo up the dread mountain, he becomes the central instrument and eventual hero of the Quest.

In their hunger and thirst and drastic deprivation, and especially in their virtual abandonment of all hope, the two hobbits traverse something akin to Christ's own *via dolorosa*, his final path of sorrow to Golgotha. Sam becomes almost a Christopher, a Christ-bearer in his portage of Frodo up the mountain. Having abandoned their mechanical defenses against evil, they also experience a virtual *noche oscura*, the black night of the soul described by the sixteenth-century Spanish mystic, St. John of the Cross. The dark night comes when, stripped of all earthly and human supports, one experiences the bracing strength of reliance on absolutely nothing other than God. "In the measure that the soul walks in darkness and emptiness in its natural operations," writes St. John, "it walks securely." Tolkien offers no such overt theological analogy, of course, but Frodo and Sam experience something akin to the Christian mystery of finding their power in their utter weakness. It is also fitting that in their trek up Mount Doom the two hobbits are sustained by nothing else than their meager portion of *lembas*, the Eucharist-like elven bread that leaves hunger frustrated but fortifies the will.

The Lust of the Eyes and Denethor's Defeatism

Concupiscence is not limited to the sins of the flesh. The eyes can lust after other things than carnal pleasures. In fact, the lust of the eyes has often been linked to an excessive desire for knowledge. Adam and Eve are filled with this sort of visual lust in their desire for the fruit of the forbidden tree, since it provides godlike knowledge. The Faustian desire for omnicompetent knowledge has often reigned as the besetting modern evil. For in our mastery of the physical universe we have presumed to have moral mastery as well. A variant of such lust for knowledge can be found in the desire to know the future and thus to obtain certainty and security. Those who despair of the ordinary assurances that are wrought by hard moral effort are often prey to this second sort of eye-lust. Hence the contemporary vogue for horoscopes, Bible-magic, and the many astrologies and psycho-therapies that feed the cravings of those who want to manage what lies ahead—the better to be rid of the unexpected and the anxiety it prompts. For then there is no need for radical reliance on God. Temperance of the eyes is thus a discipline of the soul concerning knowledge, especially knowledge of the future.

Such foresight is a dangerous thing not only for the small-souled, but also for such gallant fellows as Sam and Frodo—as they learn to their regret when they peer into the Mirror of Galadriel. The lust for knowledge of a secure future becomes all the more sinister in its effects on Denethor, the steward of Gondor. He discerns the terrible decline that has befallen his people and country, even as he also sees that the power of Mordor has been immensely strengthened. He has already lost his son Boromir in battle, and now his other son Faramir lies gravely ill, having been wounded during the retreat from Osgiliath to Minas Tirith. With good cause, it seems, Denethor perceives the future as bleak beyond bearing. He voices a repeated lament that Tolkien may have intended as a tempting dirge for our own culture and time: "The West has failed." Tolkien agreed with Oswald Spengler and many others that Western culture is caught in irrevocable decay and decline. We live in the twilight of a once-splendorous civilization, and Denethor voices our lament, even if anachronistically: "The West has failed. It shall all go up in a great fire, and all shall be ended. Ash! Ash and smoke blown away on the wind!" (3.128).

Denethor lacks the virtue of patience, the willingness to wait and work and hope for a better day. He has been using one of the *palantír*, thus enabling Sauron to give him many despairing visions of what may happen. Thinking that there is no prospect for a bright future, Denethor refuses to struggle for a gloomy but livable present. Nor does he find any comfort in the news that Aragorn, the rightful king of Gondor, is returning to ascend the throne. On the contrary, he has long known and despised him. Yet Denethor is ruined not only by his jealousy of Aragorn but also by his lustful foresight of an unendurable future. In using the seeing-stone that only a future king such as Aragorn is meant to employ, Denethor has become a defeatist—indeed, an embittered reactionary:

> "I would have things as they were in all the days of my life," answered Denethor, "and in the days of my longfathers before me: to be the Lord of this City in peace, and leave my chair to a son after me, who would be his own master and no wizard's pupil. But if doom denies this to me, then I will have *naught:* neither life diminished, nor love halved, nor honour abated." (3.130)

Unlike the despairing King Théoden, who was roused from his pessimism to help win the battle of Helm's Deep, Denethor refuses to join the fray at Pelennor Fields. His lust for a noble future has in fact maddened him. He has come to take his very nourishment from the forethought of ruin, and thus to batten on his despair. If Denethor cannot have a life as glorious as the one he once knew, he will have none at all. He tries, alas, to prevent his wounded son Faramir from facing a grim future by killing him and incinerating his body. Prevented from this frightful act of filicide, Denethor casts his own body on the funeral pyre in final suicidal despair. Such are the appalling consequences, Tolkien makes clear, of an intemperate imagination of the future, a refusal to have hope.

The Pride of Life, the Fear of Death, and the Refusal of Compromise

The Johannine phrase "the pride of life" refers to the arrogant conviction of our own self-sufficiency, the presumption that our mortal existence provides all that we need, the denial that there is anything beyond the world which would require the tempering of our earthly existence. The Ring overwhelms its victims by preying on "the pride of life," since its bearer can go on living indefinitely in apparent autonomy. According to the ancient tradition of the elves, however, death is the enormously good gift that Ilúvatar has granted humankind. Even if men had not been marred by the seductions of Melkor, they would presumably have died. But to these unfallen creatures, death would have held no terror because it would have been perceived as the blessed end of life. Men are short-lived, according to elven-lore, because their existence has been diminished by the seductions of Melkor and his minions.

There is considerable wisdom in the elven notion that death is the gift of God. For fallen creatures to go on living endlessly would be a terror to the world and a torment to themselves. We acquire wisdom, moreover, only as we live in the expectation of death—as we temper our bodily existence by not desiring falsely to prolong it. Life has its real urgency and point, Tolkien suggests, because we live toward death. If we had no prospect of dying, we would commit the two evils that undermine the good—pride and despair: pride that we will always have time to do the things that we ought to have done; despair that we will never cease doing the things we ought not to have done. The creation is good, Tolkien affirms, precisely because it is mortal. It becomes evil only when we seek to deny its mortality, either by extending our lives unnaturally or else by wasting the time that has been accorded to us.

"All we have to decide," said Gandalf, "is what to do with the time that is given us" (1.60). Far from being a *carpe diem*—a summons to seize the day for one's own self-abandoned indulgence— Gandalf echoes the urgency that runs throughout the New Testament. Repeatedly Christians are summoned not to squander their days and hours, but to be diligent in the work of the Kingdom, since "night comes, when no one can work" (John 9:4). Perhaps Gandalf's aphorism concerning time has its real roots in Paul's address to the Ephesians: "Look carefully then how you walk, not as unwise men but as wise, making the most of the time, because the days are evil" (Eph. 5:15–16). If life were to stretch on endlessly—as the Ring enables it to do—it would lose its imperative character, its urgency, its point.

The elves have not been given the benison of death; they are created as immortal beings who will never have to die—at least not until the final end of everything. Yet they have reason for growing weary of their immortality. Some of the elves, lusting after the Silmarils stolen by Melkor, decided to pursue him. Thus did they refuse to remain in Valinor, the Undying Lands that Ilúvatar prepared for them. And for this refusal they are punished with an ever-diminishing importance, so that even Galadriel's elven-status will fade once the Ring is destroyed.

Unlike the elves, men require temperance as the virtue that overcomes the temptation to prolong life endlessly. Tolkien gives us a brief glimpse of an entire civilization that succumbed to the lust for unending life, as Faramir describes the sad decline of Gondor because of its untempered fear of death. The Númenoreans had once created the most excellent of kingdoms, but they are now "a failing people." As with his father's vision of the West's decline, so with Faramir's: it has a haunting contemporary currency. We can detect our own condition in his declaration that the men of Númenor have become "Middle Men, of the Twilight, but with memory of other things . . . [W]e now love war and valour as things good in themselves, both a sport and an end" (2.287). Unlike

Denethor, however, Faramir discerns that the Men of Númenor brought their decay and dotage on themselves. In falling prey to "the pride of life," they came to revere existence itself as the ultimate good. Their worship of life and their fear of death led to a cultural degeneration not unlike our own:

> Death was ever present, because the Númenoreans . . . hungered after endless life unchanging. Kings made tombs more splendid than houses of the living, and counted old names in the rolls of their descent dearer than the names of sons. Childless lords sat in aged halls musing on heraldry; in secret chambers withered men compounded strong elixirs, or in high cold towers asked questions of the stars. And the last king of the line of Anárion had no heir. (2.286)

Those who refuse to temper "the pride of life" are tempted to another kind of death—the kind that brooks no compromise. For all that is admirable in the Ents, Tolkien reveals that they are prone—perhaps because they are so long-lived—to a deadly sufficiency. The Ents have become separated from the Entwives, and there seems to be no prospect of their reunion. The problem is that the masculine Ents are filled with wanderlust and vagabondage. They do not want to be tied down but to roam in search of ever-new things: "the Ents loved the great trees, and the wild woods, and the slopes of the high hills; and they drank of the mountain-streams, and ate only such fruit as the trees let fall in their path; and they learned of the Elves and spoke with the Trees." The Entwives, by contrast, are lovers of hearth and home, of fruits and flowers and gardens that can be tended:

> They did not desire to speak with [the wild apple and the green herbs and the seeding grasses] . . . ; but they wished them to hear and obey what was said to them. The Entwives ordered [these things] to grow according to their wishes, and bear leaf and fruit to their liking; for the Entwives desired order, and plenty, and peace (by which they meant that things should remain where they set them). (2.79)

Tolkien here offers a touching parable of the essential differences that make for tensions between men and women, husbands and wives. He is not suggesting that women have no spirit of inquiry, nor that men are incapable of a settled life. Rather is he demonstrating that our strengths, whatever they may be, always need tempering. If Ents of both genders remain incapable of compromise—not learning to put aside "the pride of life" and to honor the virtue of their opposites—they are literally doomed. There is sadness about the Ents that derives not only from their longevity but also from their solitude. They lack the cheerfulness of Sam Gamgee's self-denial. Unless both the Ents and the Entwives can temper their respective excellences, there will be no more Entings, no little Ents.

For the two kinds of tree herds again to be reunited will require far more than mere sexual mating. They will need to be reconciled. But to speak of reconciliation is to mark the limits of the cardinal virtues. Reconciliation requires more than the completion and perfection of even the most splendid moral qualities; it demands the theological gifts of faith, hope, and love. It is to the Company's embodiment of these three uniquely Christian virtues that we now turn.

Chapter Four

The Lasting Corrective:
Tolkien's Vision of the Redeemed Life

*T*he pre-Christian virtues that are common to many cultures can be magnificently perfected by divine grace. Even so, they still require a radical supplementation. There is a divine corrective that at once transforms and redeems even the best human counter-actions against evil, and it enters the world only with God's own scandalous act of self-identification in Israel and Christ. The common way of specifying the uniquely Christian virtues is to cite Paul's celebrated conclusion to 1 Corinthians 13: "So faith, hope, love abide, these three; but the greatest of these is love." The three theological virtues are not entirely distinct, of course, from the cardinal virtues—as if we were required to fulfill the four human virtues before being allowed to embark on their three divine counterparts! No aspect of human existence is devoid of God's grace; indeed, every human good is rooted in the goodness of God.

All seven of the virtues are inseparably linked, so that to sever one from the others is to do real violence to them all. We have discovered, for example, that justice requires love and mercy for its perfection, even as courage requires both faith and hope for its fulfillment. Yet the theological virtues also have their own unique qualities. It is the aim of this penultimate chapter to describe the specifically Christian character of the three theological virtues, and to show how they find indirect expression in the life and quest of the Company: *faith* in the trust that forms friendship, *hope* in the vision of a future where Good will finally prevail, and *love* in the forgiveness that is a human possibility only because it is first a divine reality. Working together to complete and perfect the classical virtues, these new virtues enable us to "become partakers of the divine nature" (2 Pet. 1:4).

Faith as Trust and Friendship

When St. Paul declares that "[h]e who through faith is righteous shall live" (Rom. 1:17) and that "by grace you have been saved through faith" (Eph. 2:8), he is not speaking of an abstract doctrine that we are called to affirm as a bare intellectual proposition. To have faith is not to credit a set of ideas that await either proof or disproof. Certainly it is true that faith has real cognitive content— namely, the articles of belief set forth in the various creeds and confessions. Summarily stated, these statements of faith affirm that the triune God has acted in Israel and Christ to create his unique people called the church and, through it, to redeem the world. Even so, faith is not the same thing as knowledge. Nor is faith something that we are required morally to do—to perform meritorious acts, for example, that win the favor of God. Surely Christian faith issues in a distinctive way of life; indeed, it is a set of habits and practices—of worship and devotion, of preaching and the sacraments. Faith is always made active and complete in good works, says the Epistle of James; in fact, "faith apart from works is dead" (Jas. 2:22, 26). Yet faith is not first of all to be understood as exemplary action.

At its root and core, faith is always an act of *trust* if it is to possess true knowledge and to produce true works. People having simple minds and accomplishing small deeds can have profound faith. Whether old or young, bright or dim, mighty or weak, we are all called to be childlike before God. Faith is the total entrustment of ourselves to the God who has trustworthily revealed himself in Israel and Christ. It is the confidence that this true God will dispose of our lives graciously, whereas we ourselves would make wretchedly ill use of them. This means that faith entails a radical risk, for God both commands and grants faith without offering any material threat of punishment or earthly promise of reward. To be sure, the life of disobedience incurs divine wrath, just as the life of faith springs from divine mercy. The right relation between God's anger and pity is defined in the fine phrase of Jeremy Taylor, a seventeenth-century Anglican divine: "God threatens terrible things if we will not be happy." To have faith is to have the life of true felicity already within us, as we learn gladly to participate in God's own trinitarian life of trusting self-surrender.

Because God's communal life centers upon the perfect and unconditional self-giving of each person of the Trinity to the other, so does the life of faith entail the complete offering of ourselves to God and our neighbors. Such an astounding act could never be a human achievement: it is a miraculous divine gift. There is nothing within our human abilities that could produce faith. On the contrary, it is our free and trusting response to the desire for God that God himself has planted within us. God is utterly unlike Melkor and Sauron because he never coerces. We are never forced but always drawn to faith, as God grants us freedom from sin's compulsion. We are invited and persuaded to this act of total entrustment through the witness to the Gospel made by the church. Even when faith is an act of knee-bent confession alone in one's own room, it is not a solitary and individual and private thing: faith is both enabled and sustained by the body of Christ called the church, the community of God's own people.

The Human Call to Faith and Trust

This brief theological discourse on faith may seem to stand at a very far remove from Tolkien. There is nothing overtly theological about *The Lord of the Rings*. The hobbits do not speak of Ilúvatar, offer sacrifices to him, or worship him in any other way. Yet it has been the central contention of this book that there are unmistakable parables and analogues of Christian faith present throughout Tolkien's masterpiece. We will see that the hobbits repeatedly find themselves performing acts of faith—entrusting themselves to each other and to their own unproven convictions about the Good—in ways that are attributable neither to human nor hobbitic powers. These faithful acts form distinctive echoes, even if at a far distance, of Christian faith.

The presence of the theological virtue of faith is made most vivid in the repeated displays of trust that constitute the real life of the Fellowship. Sometimes the hobbits are called to trust those who, like Gandalf, have discomfiting wisdom and insight. Bilbo, for example, finds it frightfully hard to surrender the Ring, so fully has it come to possess him, even though he has promised to give it up. When the old hobbit's eyes flash and harden with protective anger, Gandalf warns that he too can get furious. Yet Gandalf's moral rage is less a threat of punishment than an appeal to faith: "I am not trying to rob you, but to help you. I wish you would trust me, as you used." When Bilbo confesses that he is so torn between keeping and surrendering the Ring that he can't make up his mind, Gandalf reiterates his plea: "Then trust mine," said Gandalf. "It is quite made up. Go away and leave it behind. Stop possessing it. Give it to Frodo, and I will look after him" (1.43). This straightforward command for Bilbo to act rightly by trusting the faithful wizard breaks the spell that the Ring has worked on Bilbo, as no moral intimidation could possibly have done. Faith enables freedom.

Sam and Frodo are summoned to a similar faith when the fugitive Aragorn—disguised as a man named Strider—makes his first appearance at the inn of the Prancing Pony. The two hobbits have already encountered the foul servants of Sauron in Bree, and they thus have cause to wonder whether they can accept the uninviting Strider's claim that he has been sent by Gandalf to give them aid. Barliman Butterbur has absent mindedly failed to deliver Gandalf's letter introducing Aragorn and containing its fine paradoxical hint: *"All that is gold does not glitter, / Not all those who wander are lost."* There being no proof that Strider is in fact a king under cloak, the hobbits discover that trust is a gift that mere evidence cannot provide:

> "The lesson in caution has been well learned," said Strider with a grim smile. "But caution is one thing and wavering is another. You will never get to Rivendell now on your own, and to trust

me is your only chance. You must make up your mind. I will
answer some of your questions, if that will help you to do so.
But why should you believe my story, if you do not trust me
already?" (1.178)

Fides quaerens intellectum (faith seeking understanding) and
Credo ut intelligam (I believe that I might understand) are ancient
Christian mottoes. Though focused on faith in God, they enable
us to grasp the right relation of faith and knowledge also in the
human sphere. Trust gives birth to wisdom and understanding, as
we discover in the hobbits' first encounter with Strider. Only
because Sam and Frodo could first put their unproven faith in
Strider could they then discover his true identity. Aragorn confesses that he was indeed hoping for their trust, since it is the real
basis of friendship: "I must admit," he added with a queer laugh,
"that I hoped you would take me for my own sake. A hunted man
sometimes wearies of distrust and longs for friendship. But there,
I believe my looks are against me." Frodo admits that he had
found Strider's appearance to be forbidding, but that his intuitive
faith broke through the ugly surface to discern Aragorn's true
nobility. Frodo's faith enables him to penetrate the superficial and
to plumb real depths of character, as he confesses: "I think one of
[Sauron's] spies would—well, seem fairer and feel fouler, if you
understand" (1.183).

The Faith to Petition and Receive Divine Aid

It is not only the steadfast wizard and the fugitive king whom the
hobbits learn to trust; they also come increasingly to put their faith
in the providentially ordered universe. The hobbits have faith that
the cosmos is not accidental and absurd, not random and chaotic.
Rather is their world layered and traversed with multiple and hierarchical realities: divine, demonic, geological, zoological, botanical, elvish, human, dwarvish, hobbitic, and so on. Tolkien thus
helps us to see that our own cosmos is also a huge interstitial web
of interlocking powers. Everything—absolutely everything—
deeply intersects and overlaps with everything else. To pluck even
a single small strand of this vast cosmic web is to make the whole

thing shimmer with endless rippling effects. Yet since most of the cosmic powers are invisible, there is no proof that the world is not a godless and malign realm—a mindless universe having neither sponsorship nor direction.

The trail-blocking snowstorm that the Fellowship encounters on Mount Caradhras, for instance, seems to provide hard counter-evidence against a belief in providential order. It also disproves all notions that Tolkien was a nature worshiper. It is clear that there is a malevolent power at work in the natural order that has no link with Sauron. Thus are the hobbits required repeatedly to have faith in order to entrust themselves to Ilúvatar's cosmos. They have no sure knowledge or proof, but rather the risky confidence that Eru sponsors and directs the world, even as he enacts his will in it by means of such intermediary and intercessory agents as the unfallen and invisible valar.

Frodo and Sam are especially devoted to Elbereth, the spouse of Manwë who is also known to the elves as Gilthoniel. We have noticed earlier that she is an angelic, mercy-bearing figure with distinctive kinship to the Virgin Mary. The most remarkable fact about the hobbits' occasional petition of her aid is that they often invoke it unawares. This queen of the valar seems to be praying through *them* as much as they are praying to *her*. To use the language of the New Testament, it is as if—the hobbits being unable to pray as they ought—the Spirit were interceding for them (Rom. 8:26). When Frodo is trapped by the Barrow-wights, for example, he assumes that he has met his final end. Rather than giving up, he is angered by the wights' attack. Tolkien repeatedly resorts to the passive voice to indicate that Frodo is being graciously acted upon, even as he himself courageously acts: "He found himself stiffening" (1.151). Again when the arm of the wight draws near in the dark, Frodo discovers that "suddenly resolve hardened in him" (1.153). Unaccountably, Frodo recalls the rhyme that he had earlier learned from Tom Bombadil. Singing the verse with surprising strength—quite beyond anything he should be able to muster in his weakened condition—Frodo summons Tom to the rescue.

The synergism of the holy and the human—as the divine and the hobbitic prove to be complementary rather than contradictory—is disclosed most plainly when Frodo first encounters the Ring-wraiths. He finds himself unable to resist the inexorable urge to put on the Ring, exposing himself to the wraiths' demonic assault. With Frodo thus found out, the Witch-king bears down on the hobbit, dealing him a nearly mortal wound. Yet Frodo is saved by a surprising collusion of benign forces. Strider arrives waving a flaming brand to frighten away the light-hating wraiths, even as Frodo exerts his utmost will, both to fight the enemy and to take off the Ring. These mighty efforts succeed, however, only because another power is at work in Frodo's abject, almost unconscious petition: "At that moment [as the Witch-king was ready to strike the death blow] Frodo threw himself forward on the ground, and he heard himself crying aloud: *O Elbereth! Gilthoniel!*" (1.208). Rather than deciding to pray, Frodo discovers himself praying. As Frodo recovers from the dread blow struck by the Witch-king, Strider remarks that it was not Frodo's superb swordsmanship that really counted, since all blades perish when they pierce the lord of the Ringwraiths. "More deadly to him," Strider observes, "was the name of Elbereth" (1.210). This is far from the last occasion wherein the hobbits will entrust themselves to Elbereth's mercies. Without her aid the Quest could not have succeeded.

Because the immortal elves partake of the divine nature more fully than either hobbits or men, Galadriel the elven-queen also possesses intercessory powers. Her several gifts to the Company—the elven cloaks, the phial of light-giving water, the brooches that enable Merry and Pippin's rescue—all serve as more than mortal aids to the Quest. Galadriel also supplies the Company, far more mysteriously, with unconscious help as well. It is given almost comically when Sam is forced to surrender his elven rope as he and Frodo are making their way over the harsh ridges of Emyn Muil. Sam had tied the rope to a stump in order that he and Frodo might lower themselves down a steep cliff. There is no way, unfortunately, of untying and retrieving the rope. Sam's irritation at leaving it behind brings him as close to cursing as this guileless soul ever gets:

"Ninnyhammers!" he said. "Noodles! My beautiful rope! There it is tied to a stump, and we're at the bottom. . . . I don't like leaving it, and that's a fact." He stroked the rope's end and shook it gently. "It goes hard parting with anything I brought out of the Elf-country. Made by Galadriel herself, too, maybe. Galadriel," he murmured, nodding his head mournfully. He looked up and gave one last pull to the rope as if in farewell.

To the complete surprise of both the hobbits it came loose. (2.217)

A freak accident? A badly tied knot which, if it had given way sooner, could have spelled death? Sam knows better: "I think the rope came off itself—when I called" (2.218). The very utterance of Galadriel's name served to invoke her divine power, however little Sam intended to do so. Just as the name of Lord God must not be taken in vain—lest he fearfully perform what we lightly petition—so is it happily true with Tolkien's gracious intermediaries as well. To call upon Galadriel, even unawares, is for her to answer.

Sam's devotion to Galadriel is mystical and Marian, as Tolkien himself confessed. Gamgee hymns the beauty of the elven-princess as something verily divine—not because Galadriel is cuddly and comforting, but because her beauty is fierce and bracing. Galadriel turns Sam into a poet almost in spite of himself, as Tolkien reveals how extravagant faith in an object of worthy veneration elevates the soul of an unpretentious peasant such as Samwise Gamgee. Hence his paean of praise to his elven-lady:

"The Lady of Lórien! Galadriel!" cried Sam. "You should see her, indeed you should, sir. I am only a hobbit, and gardening's my job at home, sir, if you understand me, and I'm not much good at poetry—not at making it: a bit of comic rhyme, perhaps, now and again, you know, but not real poetry—so I can't tell you what I mean. It ought to be sung. . . . But I wish I could make a song about her. Beautiful she is, sir! Lovely! Sometimes like a great tree in flower, sometimes like a white daffadownlilly, small and slender like. Hard as di'monds, soft as moonlight. Warm as sunlight, cold as frost in the stars. Proud and far-off as a snow-mountain, and as merry as any lass I ever saw with daisies in her hair in springtime. But that's all a lot o' nonsense, and all wide of my mark."

"Then she must be lovely indeed," said Faramir. "Perilously fair."

". . . [P]erhaps you could call her perilous [Sam replies], because she's so strong in herself. You, you could dash yourself to pieces on her, like a ship on a rock; or drownd yourself, like a hobbit in a river. But neither rock nor river would be to blame." (2.288)

Galadriel bears a certain likeness to the Virgin Mary as Dante depicts her in the *Inferno*. The Blessed Maria beseeches the heavenly spirit of Beatrice Portinari, Dante's old flame, to descend from Paradise to Hell, there to persuade Virgil to rescue the wayward Dante from the damnable life that he is falling into. Here Galadriel acts without such entreaty, for she has the transcendent capacity to discern the Company's yearning as well as its need. Their faith in her leads her to protect them. Prior to the battle of Pelennor Fields, when the armies of the Free Peoples seem sure to be overwhelmed by Sauron's hugely superior forces, suddenly the fearsome Dúnedain—the mighty Men of the North—appear. Gimli assumes that Gandalf has sent for these warriors by direct word of mouth, until Legolas reminds him that the invisible elven-lady is at work:

"Nay, Galadriel," said Legolas. "Did she not speak through Gandalf of the ride of the Grey Company from the North?"

"Yes, you have it," said Gimli. "The Lady of the Wood! She read many hearts and desires." (3.49)

The Faith That Produces Friendship

The members of the Fellowship of the Ring, though they know nothing of the Greeks, are agreed with Aristotle's claim that friendship is the excellence which is "most indispensable for life." It is literally their *sine qua non*: without it they would be nothing. Their friendship is the one thing that unites them at the beginning, sustains them throughout their long ordeal, and enables the success of their Quest at the end. Friendship is surely the chief virtue of the Company. Yet because friendship is a preferential love—extended only to a few rather than to all—it has sometimes been denigrated as a sub-Christian virtue. Such castigation would be deserved only if—whether in the Company's case or our own—it led to an exclusive society of self-declared "worthy souls." The Fellowship of the Nine Walkers, quite to the contrary, is a frail and often broken community whose real bond lies in their forgiving faith and enduring trust in each other.

Friendship is born of the wondrous discovery that someone else possesses our most fundamental interests and commitments. There are evil companies, of course, formed by those who have criminal things in common. Yet, as we have discovered, there is no true community of vice, however rigidly loyal its members may be. Whether in the Taliban or the Mafia or the street gangs, their dedication to evil ends makes their singleness of spirit suffocating from within and contemptible from without. At its best, friendship constitutes a community of virtue—a fellowship of shared aims and aspirations for the Good. Unlike those who belong to a clique or in-group, friends are eager to share their common loves and enterprises with others. There is no desire to exclude outsiders who want to participate in the shared cultivation of the good thing that already-established friends have in common. As C. S. Lewis wisely remarks in *The Four Loves*, friendship is the one love that is not diminished when it is divided.

The Fellowship has its comic beginning in Sam's friendship with Frodo. Gamgee the eavesdropper overhears Gandalf telling Frodo that he must take the Ring and leave the Shire. Gandalf also urges Frodo not to make his journey alone: "Not if you know of anyone you can trust, and who would be willing to go by your side—and that you would be willing to take into unknown perils" (1.72). Having pretended to be trimming the hedge outside the window of Bag End, Sam is so overwhelmed at the thought of Frodo's leaving him that he chokes with emotion. In so small a thing as the tears of a mere gardener is so great a thing as the Fellowship initially formed. Sam fulfills, far beyond all measure, the command of Gandalf that, for the Quest, Frodo should choose a companion whom he can trust. So do Merry and Pippin, the young hobbits who insist on accompanying Frodo; they exhibit this same splendid quality of trusting friendship. Merry voices the matter simply though profoundly:

> You can trust us to stick with you through thick and thin—to the bitter end. And you can trust us to keep any secret of yours—closer than you keep it yourself. But you cannot trust us to let you face trouble alone, and go off without a word. We are your friends, Frodo. (1.115–16)

With those last five words, had Sauron heard and fathomed them, his mighty fortress at Barad-dûr would have been shaken to its foundations.

Noble as their friendship surely is, it will never depend on heroic deeds alone. The Fellowship will also be sustained by acts that are wonderfully comic and only inadvertently heroic. Chasing the fleeing Frodo after Boromir attempts to seize the Ring, bumbling Sam misses Frodo's departing boat by several feet. As he falls into the river and nearly drowns, Gamgee all the while exclaims, "Coming, Mr. Frodo! Coming!" Sam may be clumsy and comical and inept, but his loyalty to Frodo defines the real character of the Company:

> "Of all the confounded nuisances you are the worst, Sam!" [Frodo] said.
>
> "Oh, Mr. Frodo, that's hard!" said Sam shivering. "That's hard, trying to go without me and all. If I hadn't a guessed right, where would you be now?"
>
> "Safely on my way."
>
> "Safely!" said Sam. "All alone and without me to help you? I couldn't have a borne it, it'd have been the death of me."
>
> "It would be the death of you to come with me, Sam," said Frodo, "and I couldn't have borne that." (1.422)

The Nine Walkers are chosen by Elrond as Middle-earth's answer to the Nine Riders of Sauron—the nine mortal men who, wearing the rings that Sauron made for them, have come totally under his power and thus have been turned into the fearsome Ringwraiths. But while the Nine Riders have been made into vaporous shadows of sameness, the Nine Walkers are a remarkably diverse assemblage of the unlike. They represent all of the Free Peoples of

Middle-earth, and they are not united by race or language or class, but solely by their friendship: their abiding love for each other and their common devotion to the Good as it is embodied in the Quest. Together, these two things give them an immense moral freedom, and thus an immense power against Sauron, the Ringwraiths, and all the other enemies of such freedom.

Elrond chooses these radically disparate souls according to the unique strengths they bring to their singular task. Their unity in drastic unlikeness makes the Fellowship a startling analogue of what the New Testament calls "one body and one Spirit, . . . one hope . . . one Lord, one faith, one baptism, one God and Father of us all" (Eph. 4:4–6). Gandalf is chosen for his wisdom, Aragorn because of his ancestral link to the Ring, Boromir for his valor, Legolas for his elvish mastery of the woods, Gimli for his dwarvish knowledge of mountains and mines, and Sam because he is Frodo's closest companion. Merry and Pippin are selected, despite their youthful inexperience, because they are eager to follow Frodo. When Elrond objects that these youngsters have no ability to imagine the terrors that lie ahead, Gandalf reminds him that they possess a more important quality: "It is true that if these hobbits understood the danger, they would not dare go. But they would still wish to go, or wish that they dared, and be shamed and unhappy. I think, Elrond, that in this matter it would be well to trust rather to their friendship than to great wisdom" (1.289).

The four hobbits are already friends, but the other five members of the Company soon join them in an unbreakable circle of faith and trust and solidarity. They are united by their common purpose, by their loyalty to Gandalf as their guide, by their hatred of Sauron and all his pomps, by their desire to preserve Middle-earth from destruction and, increasingly, by their mutual sacrifice and suffering. These qualities are not uniquely Christian, of course, but have their parallels in pagan societies as well. It has often been noted that, under the actual conditions of war, few soldiers fight for such an abstract and distant good as their nation or people, but rather for the concrete and immediate good of their soldier friends.

Tolkien adds one distinctive quality to the faith that binds the

Fellowship, and this makes it deeply analogous to the life of authentic Christian community. In the heroic world of the ancient North, warriors were made to swear absolute fealty, even on pain of death, against betrayal of their common cause. The Company, by contrast, is not required to take an oath. Perhaps Tolkien here echoes Christ's own prohibition against oath-swearing (Matt. 5:33–35). Whether with hobbits or humans, oaths often bind rather than free the will, allowing room for neither failure nor forgiveness. The Fellowship depends on the liberating faith and grace of friendship, not on the forced loyalty of oaths:

> "This is my last word," [Elrond] said in a low voice. "The Ring-bearer is setting out on the Quest of Mount Doom. On him alone is any charge laid: neither to cast away the Ring, nor to deliver it to any servant of the Enemy nor indeed to let any handle it, save members of the Company and the Council, and only then in gravest need. The others go with him as free companions, to help him on his way. You may tarry, or come back, or turn aside into other paths, as chance allows. The further you go, the less easy will it be to withdraw; yet no oath or bond is laid on you to go further than you will. For you do not yet know the strength of your hearts, and you cannot foresee what each may meet upon the road." (1.294)

The solidarity of the Company is first evidenced as they are entering Lothlórien. Because dwarves and elves have been historic enemies, the guardian Haldir demands that Gimli be blindfolded before entering the elven-realm. Gimli defends his innocence, pointing out that he has never served Sauron nor done any harm to elves. It is Aragorn, however, who makes the salient point. The question is not whether Gimli is an enemy of elves, Aragorn argues, but whether the Nine Walkers really constitute a Fellowship. Either they shall *all* enter Lórien blindfolded, Aragorn insists, or else *none* of them shall be hindered (1.362).

St. Paul speaks very much in Elrond's fashion when he emphasizes the unity of all members of Christ's body. Each person—no matter how small or "inferior"—is essential for the solidarity of the whole: "If one member suffers, all suffer together; if one member is honored, all rejoice together" (1 Cor. 12:26). There are few evils that do more harm to the Gospel than the division of Christians against each other. Haldir confesses the hard truth about schisms, whether churchly or hobbitic, when he admits that his initial suspicion of Gimli was prompted by the enmity that Sauron himself has sown: "Indeed in nothing is the power of the Dark Lord more clearly shown than in the estrangement that divides all those who still oppose him" (1.362). Knowing the true identity and purpose of the Company, Galadriel permits them all alike to enter freely.

Surely the most remarkable friendship within the Company itself is the one that develops between Gimli and Legolas. Dwarves and elves have little in common. While dwarves delve deep into the innards of the earth, elves are masters of trees and woods. Yet this racial divide does not hinder the regard that Gimli and Legolas come to have for each other. Perhaps angered at Gimli's having been denied an open-eyed entrance to Lórien, Legolas befriends the dwarf there in the elven-world. Their friendship is further strengthened at the battle of Helm's Deep. After the final fight before the Black Gate of Mordor, the elf and dwarf renew their vow never to let their companionship be broken. Thus does Gimli promise to journey with Legolas to the Forest of Fangorn, there to behold the wonders of this fairest of elven places; just as Legolas pledges to accompany Gimli to the caves beneath Helm's Deep, there to enjoy the glories of the dwarf mines.

In appendix A of *The Lord of the Rings*, we learn something even more wondrous about the friendship of Gimli and Legolas. After spending much time and labor rebuilding ruined Gondor, and after viewing the wonders of Middle-earth together, they were *both* allowed to sail over the sea to Valinor (3.362). Their friendship made their parting so unbearable that Galadriel seems to have interceded with the valar on Gimli's behalf. He thus becomes the only dwarf ever to have entered the Undying Lands. Yet this is no unvarnished reward for Gimli. He must forgo a long and glorious rest with his ancestors. Yet Gimli gladly makes this sacrifice in order to remain, until the end of Time, with his best friend as well as the Lady whom he cherishes above all the precious metals that he has quarried and refined.

The Dangers of Suspicion and the Spoiling of Friendship

Galadriel predicts that the Fellowship, being a body of true friends, will enlarge its periphery by meeting unexpected friends along their journey. And indeed it does: Bombadil and Treebeard, Théoden and Erestor, Éomer and Éowyn are but the most obvious examples. Yet while friendship may bring forth wonders, it can also create disasters. Friendship loses its virtue when others are not welcomed into its circle—when its preferential love produces a clique or in-group. The Company would not seem to be afflicted with a partisan denial of friendship to others but, in one notable instance, it is.

Gandalf taught Frodo to forgive the utterly undeserving Gollum, even as Bilbo had done. And once Frodo saw the pathetically shriveled and twisted figure, he gladly granted him mercy. As himself a bearer of the Ring for only a short time, Frodo understands how hideous was the pressure that bore down on Gollum for all the years that he possessed it. Frodo knows that, unless he resists relentlessly, he will become his own version of Gollum. Thus does Frodo come gradually but increasingly to trust him. Frodo does not extend Gollum the faith that comes with full friendship, of course. For in his mad desire to reclaim the Ring, Gollum is eminently untrustworthy. Frodo insists that, when he is sleeping, Sam must keep an eye on the treacherous hobbit. Even so, Frodo has a strange respect for Gollum. He discerns, in a deeply intuitive way, that Gollum is divinely destined to play his crucial role in the saga of the Ring. Far more importantly, Frodo believes that Gollum is not fixed in evil, but that he has the capacity to overcome the addictive effects of the Ring. He wants, therefore, to extend at least minimal friendship to this miserable fellow hobbit. There is a tiny ray of light peeking into the prison cell of Gollum's life, making him long to leave his wretched isolation and to find companionship with another creature of his own kind.

Sam's moral imagination is far too limited to discern Gollum's desire, and this blinkered failure of faith also marks Sam's real failure in friendship. Sam's problem springs, at least in part, from his hyper-cautious peasant mentality. His simple mind is accustomed to dealing in moral simplicities rather than complexities: everything is either good or bad, and Gollum is bad. This judgment is largely true, of course. Nowhere does Tolkien suggest that Gollum has anything other than a corrupt character. Even so, it is evident that Sam is determined not to find even a sliver of good in Gollum. He treats him with utter contempt, repeatedly calling him a "nasty treacherous creature" (2.224), and giving him multiple unsavory names: "Slinker" and "Stinker" and "Sneak." Sam's revulsion for Gollum—his cold scorn rather than his hot hatred—is evident from the moment Sam first spies him at the edge of the Dead Marshes:

> [Gollum's] large head on its scrawny neck was lolling from side to side as if he was listening. His pale eyes were half unlidded. Sam restrained himself, though his fingers were twitching. [Sam's] eyes, filled with anger and disgust, were fixed on the wretched creature as he now began to move again, still whispering and hissing to himself. (2.220)

Tolkien's narrator calls the untrustworthy hobbit a "wretched creature." Frodo employs the same sympathetic epithet to describe Gollum: "If we kill him, we must kill him outright. But we can't do that, not as things are. Poor wretch! He has done us no harm" (2.221).

Perhaps because Frodo treats him in a civil and polite fashion, Gollum begins to recover his freedom, his Sméagol self. Frodo calls forth Gollum's best traits by refusing to focus on his worst ones. Tolkien thus echoes what, in his *Confessions*, St. Augustine says about God's own love for him: "In loving me, You made me lovable." In response to Frodo's faith in him, Gollum begins to speak in the first person singular, and he swears never to let Sauron have the Ring—a promise that, in fact, he never breaks. Frodo is able to engage Gollum sympathetically because they share the same experience of the Ring's burden. Oddly and profoundly, it is their suffering that prompts their potential communion: "the two were in some way akin and not alien: they could reach one another's minds" (2.225).

Frodo's kind desire to enter Gollum's inner life is totally alien to Sam. He would be much happier if Gollum remained wholly evil: "[Sam] suspected him more deeply than ever, and if possible liked the new Gollum, the Sméagol, less than the old" (2.225). The narrator is candid about the sinister effects of Sam's blindness toward Gollum: "Sam's mind was occupied mostly with his master, hardly noticing the dark cloud that had fallen on his own heart" (2.238). Sam is intensely jealous of any rivals to Frodo's friendship. As Frodo's boon companion, he wants his master to have no other. Thus does Sam seek to shrink the circle of intimate community to the smallest possible circumference. This is the spoiling of faithful friendship.

Frodo is not deluded that Gollum has somehow suddenly become virtuous, but he nonetheless decides to put his faith in Gollum to lead them into Mordor rather than thinking only evil of him: "I will trust you once more. Indeed it seems that I must do so, and that it is my fate to receive help from you, where I least looked for it, and [it is] your fate to help me whom you long pursued with evil purpose" (2.248). Again at the Forbidden Pool, when Faramir and Samwise would have killed Gollum for his deadly trespass, Frodo rescues him. That he must resort to trickery to persuade Gollum to leave the pool is a considerable grief to Frodo. He despises using treachery even against the treacherous. Frodo thus rejects Faramir's insistence that he should not trust Gollum to show them the path to Mordor. Even the faithless should be shown faith: "I have promised many times to take [Gollum] under my protection and to go where he led. You would not ask me to break faith with him?" (2.301)

Sam is quite glad to break faith with Gollum—convinced as he is that Gollum should *never* be trusted. But as Gamgee's moral discernment deepens, he discovers that Gollum is a morally complex creature. As Sam puts it, Gollum is *both* Stinker (rotten with desire for the Ring) and Slinker (stealthy in his movements and motives). Gollum's conflicted nature becomes especially evident in his fierce inner debates concerning his temptation to seize the Ring from Frodo. In the first of these interior arguments, he resists the lure of the Ring, as if the power of good were gradually winning out. In the second and last one, Gollum finds both Sam and Frodo asleep. It is an apt occasion for Gollum to work his malice and greed.

Instead, he approaches Frodo with an apparent desire for communion. He seems to understand that Frodo has trusted him again and again—not out of mere necessity, but in a desire for friendship. Describing the scene from a transcendent perspective, the narrator treats Gollum with remarkable tenderness:

> [S]lowly putting out a trembling hand, very cautiously [Gollum] touched Frodo's knee—but almost the touch was a caress. For a fleeting moment, could one of the sleepers have seen him, they would have thought that they beheld an old weary hobbit, shrunken by the years that had carried him far beyond his time, beyond fields and kin, and the fields and streams of youth, an old starved pitiable thing. (2.324)

In a moment of exceeding ill fortune, Frodo stirs in his sleep—perhaps responding to a nightmare—at the very moment Gollum touches him. His cry in turn awakens the much-alarmed Sam, who immediately suspects the worst of Gollum, calling him "you old villain." Once Sam sees that Gollum meant Frodo no harm, he apologizes for having wrongly accused him. But it is too late. Gollum uses Sam's taunt as an excuse to return to his old self: "Almost spider-like he looked now, crouched back on his bent limbs, with his protruding eyes. The fleeting moment had passed, beyond recall" (2.324). Tolkien confessed that this inopportune turn of events saddened him immensely—as Gollum comes ever so close to a healing of his riven soul, only to be balked by Frodo's sudden awakening and Sam's sharp rebuke (L, 110).

Yet Tolkien's lament may have also been pointed at Sam. For in his jealous refusal to extend even the most minimal friendship to Gollum, Gamgee has given him ample pretext for suppressing his free Sméagol self and for returning to his enslaved condition as Gollum. At the end, when it is again too late, Sam does forgive Gollum. Even so, the lesson has been well learned: to expect evil of others, Tolkien suggests in accord with Scripture, is to call out their worst rather than their best selves. Hence the constant biblical command not to think well of oneself and ill of one's fellows, but to accord them generosity and goodwill. A right estimate of others, according to St. Paul, can be obtained only by regarding them no longer from a human point of view, but rather by beholding them as creatures for whom Christ has died (2 Cor. 5:16).

No such recourse, we hardly need to observe, is possible to any of Tolkien's characters. Thus must our judgment of Sam remain within the limits of his own moral and spiritual world. Sam redeems much of what he has lost in his distrust of Gollum by his unfailing loyalty to Frodo. He befriends Frodo in nearly every possible way. And at the end, he virtually surrenders his own life in Frodo's behalf. Though himself weak and weary from the many vicissitudes of their journey, Sam finds himself surprisingly able to carry Frodo the last miles up Mount Doom: "Sam lifted Frodo with no more difficulty than if he were carrying a hobbit-child pig-a-back in some romp on the lawns or hayfields of the Shire" (3.218). The narrator admits that Frodo has been rendered light by his wasting wounds and sorrows, but another paradox is also at work: when doing the most difficult things for the sake of the Good, they become astonishingly effortless. "My yoke is easy, and my burden is light" (Matt. 11:30).

Nor is Tolkien squeamish about having Sam express his love for Frodo physically, as he kisses Frodo's hands, holds the sleeping Frodo's head in his lap, and places his own hand on the somnolent Frodo's breast. Whether in ancient hyper-masculine cultures or modern homoerotic cultures, such gestures are suspect. Not for Tolkien. Instead, he depicts Sam and Frodo's friendship as a thing of exquisite beauty, even holiness. The most poignant account of their *philia* is found in the fair land of Ithilien, where they have come after having been turned away at the Black Gate of Mordor. Sam beholds the sleeping Frodo as a friend whose worth is beyond all estimate:

> He was reminded suddenly of Frodo as he had lain, asleep in the house of Elrond, after his deadly wound. Then as he had kept watch Sam had noticed that at times a light seemed to be shining faintly within; but now the light was even clearer and stronger. Frodo's face was peaceful, the marks of fear and care had left it; but it looked old, old and beautiful, as if the chiseling of the shaping years was now revealed in many fine lines that

had before been hidden, though the identity of the face was not changed. Not that Sam Gamgee put it that way to himself. He shook his head, as if finding words useless, and murmured: "I love him. He's like that, and sometimes it shines through, somehow. But I love him, whether or no." (2.260)

These sentiments, felt and spoken at the edge of Mordor, reveal the ultimate distance between the Fellowship and their enemies. None of Sauron's slaves can be imagined as ever uttering such a simple sentence as "I love him." Sam and Frodo give incarnate life to what the Old Testament means when it describes a friend as a person "who is as your own soul" (Deut. 13:6). Their mutual regard is also akin to the friendship of Jonathan and David: "the soul of Jonathan was knit to the soul of David, and Jonathan loved him as his own soul" (1 Sam. 18:1). So is their bond like that between the veteran missionary and his younger colleague: "I thank God . . . when I remember you constantly in my prayers. As I remember your tears, I long night and day to see you, that I may be filled with joy" (2 Tim. 1:3–4).

Together with all the other members of the Company, Sam has fulfilled the command of the Christ whom he knows not: "Greater love has no man than this, that a man lay down his life for his friends" (John 15:13). Sam's faith in Frodo results in a friendship like few others in ancient or modern literature. Though Sam sees himself as Frodo's servant above all else, he would understand— at least by the end—what Frodo would mean if he were thus to address the Fellowship: "No longer do I call you servants . . . but I have called you friends" (John 15:15). Faithful friendship within the Company measures the chasm between the two worlds that *The Lord of the Rings* sets in startling opposition: the world of life and the world of death.

Hope in a Future That Is Permanently Good

Tolkien is candid about the bleak character of pagan heroism: it is literally hopeless. Speaking of the Anglo-Saxon world of *Beowulf*, he confessed that "those days were heathen—heathen, noble, and hopeless" (MC, 22). They were hopeless because not even the gods could overcome the powers of Chaos and Unreason. Beowulf and his allies struggled with absolutely no hope of winning in the end, even if they were temporarily to defeat the monsters. Even if they were victorious and won the glory that they sought, their final destruction could not be averted. Yet this defeat was no refutation of their cause. On the contrary, their highest vindication lay in standing up to the fiends, knowing well that they could be devoured by them and that, even if not, their own extinction was still sure.

A kindred hopelessness makes its way into *The Lord of the Rings*. After Gandalf has been slain by the Balrog, for example, Aragorn voices the grim situation of the whole Company: "We must do without hope," he said. "At least we may yet be avenged. Let us gird ourselves and weep no more! Come! We have a long road, and much to do" (1.347). When Aragorn departs for the Paths of the Dead, seeking to rouse the disembodied spirits of the Shadow Host to battle the Corsairs of Umbar, there is little expectation that he might succeed. Again when the combined armies of the Free Peoples make their assault on the Black Gate of Mordor, they have no hope whatsoever that they will win. Yet it is Frodo himself who is most often overwhelmed by hopelessness. As the Ring continues to work its sinister pressures on him, he feels increasingly helpless to resist it. Hence Sam's despairing confession as he debates with himself about their prospects:

> It's all quite useless. . . . You are the fool, [Sam,] going on hop-
> ing and toiling. You could have lain down and gone to sleep
> together [with Frodo] days ago, if you hadn't been so dogged.
> But you'll die just the same, or worse. You might just as well lie
> down now and give it up. You'll never get to the top anyway.
> (3.216)

Sam refuses to surrender to such hopelessness. Instead, he carries Frodo all the way to the summit of the volcanic mountain. There Frodo exerts his utmost—albeit finally insufficient—energy against Sauron. They both go on "hoping and toiling" without any reason other than the worthiness of their Quest. Yet their determination is not entirely hopeless and their heroism is not entirely pagan. On at least three occasions, they receive a glimpse of the transcendent hope that assures the ultimate success of their Quest.

Hope Brought by the Return of the True King

Aragorn is a central member of the Fellowship because he is the heir of Isildur, the king who had seized the Ring from Sauron by cutting it off his finger. Aragorn also wields Isildur's once-broken sword that has now been reforged, an instrument not only of great power but also of true authority. With Éomer succeeding Théoden as king of Rohan, and thus with the maintenance of royal rule, the elves have hope that Moria will be protected from the ravages of Sauron. But the northwestern lands of Middle-earth will be well ruled only if Aragorn also returns as king of Gondor and Arnor. The hobbits also have much at stake in Aragorn's rightful resumption of his kingship, since the Shire is part of Arnor, and since Mordor borders on Gondor. Evil is never a spiritual or disembodied reality in Tolkien's work; it is a political, social, and geographical threat.

The hobbits themselves have no need of a ruler, since they live in splendid concord—with the exception of such family rivalries as the one between the Bagginses and the Sackville-Bagginses! They have no written laws, no police (except for a Shirriff or two, as well as the Bounders who patrol the borders of the Shire), nor any civic officers except for the mayor. Even so, the residents of Hobbiton and Bree have a huge investment in Aragorn's return as king, since he will prohibit all human intrusions into the Shire, this last little corner of unspoiled life within Middle-earth.

With this exception, Tolkien held that all other peoples require a just ruler. Both as a monarchist and a Christian, he held that the good king (or the good queen) is the representative ideal citizen: the person who, by virtue of lineage and office, represents the people at their best, fulfilling their noblest possibilities. For a good monarch to reign, it follows, is for the entire people to be exalted, even—indeed, especially—the lowliest. It is noteworthy that Aragorn seeks to rescue the youngest and most vulnerable members of the Fellowship, Merry and Pippin, when they are captured by orcs. He seeks the good of the small no less than the great.

A rightful ruler such as Aragorn does not have symbolic power alone. His majesty's government is obliged to promote the commonweal in the most important ways: to curtail the evils that undermine a just society and to promote the goods that sustain it. To have no true and just ruler is, by contrast, to suffer the worst of all calamities. It means that the people have no real life. True existence, whether ancient or modern, is never merely private but also and always public; it is found in the *polis*—the city or the village. For these reasons, the political question—the question of the rightly ordered civic realm—always looms large in *The Lord of the Rings*. The crowning of Aragorn is, in many ways, the climactic moment of the novel.

Though first disguised as Strider, lest his true identity be found out and he be thwarted in reclaiming his kingship, Aragorn gradually makes evident his right to the office. When he first confronts Éomer to ask for his help, Aragorn declares his royal status as the heir of Elendil and Isildur. What would seem vain and arrogant to an egalitarian world such as ours is, for Tolkien, the essence of real authority:

> Aragorn threw back his cloak. The elven-sheath glittered as he grasped it, and the bright blade of Andúril shone like sudden flame as he swept it out. "Elendil," he cried. "I am Aragorn son of Arathorn, and am called Elessar, the Elfstone, Dúnadan, the heir of Isildur Elendil's son of Gondor. Here is the Sword that was Broken and is forged again! Will you aid me or thwart me? Choose swiftly!" (2.36)

Aragorn's kingly powers are also made evident when Pippin foolishly seizes the *palantír* at Isengard. Gandalf charges Aragorn to take ownership of it despite the danger. "Dangerous indeed, but not to all," said Aragorn. "There is one who may claim it by right. For this assuredly is the *palantír* of Orthanc from the treasury of Elendil, set here by the Kings of Gondor. Now my hour draws near. I will take it. . . . That hour is now come, I think" (2.199–200). Aragorn replies in terms that seem deliberately to echo Jesus' own approach to Golgotha, where he would also be crowned king, albeit of a radically different kind (Mark 14:26).

Aragorn displays his wisdom—and thus his desire to give the Company hope—by using the *palantír* to expose himself to Sauron. He does not reveal himself merely as a man named Strider, but as the king and ruler of Gondor and Arnor, and thus as the heir of Elendil and Isildur: "To know that I lived and walked the earth was a blow to his heart. . . . Sauron has not forgotten Isildur and the sword of Elendil. Now in the very hour of his great designs the heir of Isildur and the Sword are revealed, for I showed the blade re-forged to him. He is not so mighty yet that he is above fear; nay, doubt ever gnaws him" (3.53–54). Sauron is bitten with worry not only because Aragorn is mighty but also because he is righteous: regal goodness is a dire threat to the prince of evil. And in turning all of his wrath on Aragorn at the Black Gate, Sauron was distracted from noticing the presence of Sam and Frodo as they clawed their way up his own infernal mountain.

Aragorn embodies hope even in his name. We are told in appendix A that, while he was called Aragorn by his mother, he had been raised in Rivendell by the elves as Estel, which means "Hope" (3.338). Gandalf repeatedly uses the word "hope" when speaking of Aragorn, just as he also employs the returning king's own prophetic language to describe him: "His time draws near" (3.88). Aragorn's right to rule is supremely manifest in his having roused and redeemed the Shadow Host to defeat Sauron's buccaneers at the haven of Pelargir, and then in leading the assembled forces of the Free Peoples against Sauron's forces in the victory at Pelennor Fields. In the midst of that fray, Aragorn meets Éomer who, like him, is an uncrowned king. But rather than regarding each other as rivals, "they leaned on their swords and looked on one another and were glad" (3.123).

It becomes ever more evident that Aragorn's kingship is theological as well as political. Since in Middle-earth there is no church with elders or bishops or other religious authorities, Tolkien gives spiritual power to his monarchs. This is no anomaly. Medieval kings, ruling by divine right rather than democratic election, were believed to have supernatural powers of healing. Thus does

Aragorn heal the wounded Éowyn and Faramir—using both his careful knowledge of herb lore as well as his majestic presence—after they have both been gravely wounded at the battle of Pelennor Fields. An aphorism from ancient tradition thus proves prophetic, as Ioreth, a wise woman of Gondor, declares: *"The hands of the king are the hands of a healer, and so shall the rightful king be known"* (3.139).

The attack led by Aragorn on the Black Gate of Mordor seems quite hopeless. Even with their army of ten thousand, the amassed forces of the Free Peoples are but grist for Sauron's military machine, the hosts of Mordor. As Aragorn instructs his soldiers before the battle, therefore, he speaks with the realism of a true king, refusing to goad them with either heroic promises of victory or equally heroic assurances of defeat: "We come now to the very brink, where hope and despair are akin. To waver is to fall" (3.156). When Prince Imrahil, one of the bravest Captains of the West, suggests that Sauron will laugh in his scorn for the pitiful armies assaulting his Black Gate, Aragorn insists that this final battle is no laughing matter. They have come to do their duty, in the hope that their Quest will be vindicated, whether they triumph or are slaughtered:

> "If this be jest, then it is too bitter for laughter. Nay, it is the last move in a great jeopardy, and for one side or other it will bring the end of the game." Then he drew Andúril and held it up glittering in the sun. "You shall not be sheathed again until the last battle is fought," he said. (3.158)

The armies of the West are indeed on the brink of defeat when suddenly a huge shadow, like "a vast threatening hand," reaches out of Mordor toward them, "terrible but impotent," and then vanishes, blown away by the wind (3.227). Sauron's forces flee in horror, we know, because Gollum has tumbled into the Cracks of Mount Doom and melted the Ring, at the same time destroying Sauron and robbing his minions of all their might. The Sauronic soldiers had fought in fear and loathing of their master, yet in sure confidence of victory. Now they have neither cause to prod them, and so they flee in terror. Yet the victory over Sauron that is won with the destruction of the

Ring will not have its earthly realization until Lord Aragorn has been crowned king, for only when right political order has been re-established can true hope be restored.

In a scene of elaborate pomp and magnificent ceremony, Faramir the Steward of Gondor welcomes Aragorn to Minas Tirith for his coronation. But when Faramir offers the crown to Aragorn, he declines to make himself king. This is a remarkable departure from ancient custom, where the king often elevated himself as lord over all others in an act of self-investiture. Instead, Aragorn hands the crown back to Faramir, insisting that he give it to Frodo the Ring-bearer, who in turn will give it to Gandalf for the actual coronation. By means of this remarkable chain of deference, Aragorn honors the noblest of the mortal and supermortal creatures to whom he owes his restored kingship: the lowly hobbit who bore the Ring back to Mount Doom, and the great wizard who guided them all along their Quest.

After Aragorn kneels to receive the crown from Gandalf, and then rises to his feet, there is a hugely significant pause. The regal celebrations begin only after the people have witnessed a virtual epiphany, a revelation of their king as more than an earthly ruler—as their true lord and master. Because Aragorn is disclosed as their rightful king, they are able also to behold what they themselves are at their best. Tolkien borrows metaphors from both Testaments (Dan. 7:9; John 19:14) to hymn the transcendent glory and hope embodied in Aragorn's kingship:

> [W]hen Aragorn arose all that beheld him gazed in silence, for it seemed to them that he was revealed to them now for the first time. Tall as the sea-kings of old, he stood above all that were near; ancient of days he seemed and yet in the flower of manhood; and wisdom sat upon his brow, and strength and healing were in his hands, and a light was about him. And then Faramir cried:
> "Behold the King!" (3.246)

Hope beyond the Walls of the World

Although Aragorn's wedding to Arwen soon follows his crowning as king, and although he undertakes a massive reconstruction program to recover the lost splendor of Arnor and Gondor, we learn in *The History of Middle-earth* that Aragorn was succeeded by unworthy kings. The hope engendered by the reign of a true king, Tolkien reveals, cannot finally suffice. Nor do the lives of Aragorn and Arwen themselves end happily. On the contrary, they are immensely sad. Aragorn elects to die of his own will rather than to dodder off into senility and misrule. Enabling his well-prepared son Eldarion to succeed to the throne, Aragorn lays "himself down after the manner of the ancient kings of Númenor, and died, in the hundred and second year of his reign and the hundred and nineti- eth year of his life" (PM, 244). Aragorn's parting words to Arwen are poignant indeed: "In sorrow we must go, but not in despair. Behold! we are not bound for ever to the circles of the world, and beyond them is more than memory. Farewell!" (3.344).

What this "beyond" might mean is already implicit in the death of Aragorn. His corpse is virtually beatified, as if his body were imbued with the same glory and sanctity that were disclosed at his coronation: "Then a great beauty was revealed in him, so that all who came after there looked on him in wonder; for they saw that the grace of his youth, and the valour of his manhood, and the wis- dom and majesty of his age were blended together. And long there he lay, an image of the splendour of the Kings of Men in glory undimmed before the breaking of the world" (3.344). Having grown "cold and grey as nightfall in winter that comes without a star," Arwen soon chooses to follow Aragorn, surrendering her elven immortality to be joined with him in death. The description of her burial contains another hint of resurrection: "[S]he laid her- self to rest upon Cerin Amroth; and there is her green grave, until the world is changed." This is the same phrase that we have already encountered in *The Hobbit*, as Tolkien obliquely suggests, yet again, a hope for radically renewed life beyond "the circles of the world."

Christian hope concerns precisely this radical change that breaks the cycle of the world's endless turning. It takes the natural human aspiration to happiness and reorders it to the Kingdom of heaven. Such hope is not a general optimism about the nature of things, nor a forward-looking confidence that all will eventually be well. Instead, it is hope in a future that God alone both can and will provide. "For thou, O Lord, art my hope, my trust, O LORD, from my youth" (Ps. 71:5). "Behold, the eye of the LORD is on those who fear him, on those who hope in his steadfast love, that he may deliver their soul from death, and keep them alive in famine" (Ps. 33:18–19). The radically future-oriented character of Christian hope—the conviction that salvation in this life is never complete—can hardly be denied. Christian hope springs from the faith that what God has begun in Israel and Christ, he will consummate on the Last Day. This hope of eternal beatitude preserves Christians from discouragement, sustains them when they have been abandoned, protects them from the selfishness of despair, and prompts them to acts of charity. It gives faith its real motive force:

> [T]he creation was subjected to futility, not of its own will but by the will of him who subjected it in hope; because the creation itself will be set free from its bondage to decay and obtain the glorious liberty of the children of God. We know that the whole creation has been groaning in travail together until now; and not only the creation, but we ourselves, who have the first fruits of the Spirit, groan inwardly as we wait for adoption as sons, the redemption of our bodies. For in this hope we were saved. Now hope that is seen is not hope. For who hopes for what he sees? But if we hope for what we do not see, we wait for it with patience. (Rom. 8:20–25)

While it is impossible for any member of the Company ever to voice such a distinctively Christian hope, they all stake their lives on a future realization of the Good beyond the bounds of the world. We have seen repeatedly how their devotion to the Quest does not depend upon any sort of certainty concerning its success. They are called to be faithful rather than victorious. Often the Fellowship finds its profoundest hope when the prospects seem bleakest.

Near the end of their wearying journey, Frodo and Sam are alone, deep within Mordor, crawling like mere insects across a vast wilderness. All their efforts seem finally to have failed. Even if somehow they succeed in destroying the Ring, there is no likelihood that they will survive, or that anyone will ever hear of their valiant deed. They seem doomed to oblivion. Yet amidst such apparent hopelessness, Sam—the peasant hobbit who, despite his humble origins, has gradually emerged as a figure of great moral and spiritual insight—beholds a single star shimmering above the dark clouds of Mordor:

> The beauty of it smote his heart, as he looked up out of the forsaken land, and hope returned to him. For like a shaft, clear and cold, the thought pierced him that in the end the Shadow was only a small and passing thing: there was light and high beauty for ever beyond its reach. His song in the Tower [of Cirith Ungol] had been defiance rather than hope; for then he was thinking of himself. Now, for a moment, his own fate, and even his master's, ceased to trouble him. He crawled back into the brambles and laid himself by Frodo's side, and putting away all fear he cast himself into a deep and untroubled sleep. (3.199)

This meditation is noteworthy on several counts. Fearing Gollum's treachery, Sam has never before allowed himself to sleep while Frodo also slept. That he should do so now is a sign of transcendent hope—the conviction, namely, that their ultimate well-being lies beyond any foiling of it by Gollum's deceit or Sauron's sorcery. For Sam the consummate loyalist not to be vexed by Frodo's fate is for him to have found hope in a future that will last, no matter the outcome of their errand. More remarkable still is Sam's discernment of the relative power of good and evil, light and darkness, life and death, hope and despair. The vast darkened sky of Mordor, illumined by only a single star, would seem to signal the triumph of evil once and for all. Yet Sam is not bound by the logic of the obvious. He sees that star and shadow are not locked in a dualistic combat of equals, nor are they engaged in a battle whose outcome remains uncertain. He discerns the deep and paradoxical truth that the dark has no meaning apart from the light. Light is both the primal and the final reality, not the night that seeks to quench it. The single flickering star, Sam sees, penetrates and defines the gargantuan gloom. "The light shines in the darkness, and the darkness has not overcome it" (John 1:5).

Sam's metaphysical insight, excellent though it is, cannot be sustained apart from a Fellowship such as the nine friends have formed and a Quest such as they have been charged to fulfill. It also requires a sustaining Story—one that is rooted in their history and that sums up and embodies not only their own struggle against Sauron but also the struggle of all the Free Peoples of Middle-earth against similar evils. The Jews repeatedly rehearse the story of their deliverance from Egyptian bondage as the single narrative of Yahweh's election and formation of Israel to be his own people. It is their means of keeping their own hope alive amidst exile and defeat. So it is with Christians. In both its preaching and sacraments, in its creeds and hymns and prayers, the church rehearses its founding and shaping Story—the account of God's act in the life and death and resurrection and return of Jesus Christ—as the one abiding hope not only for the church but also for the whole world.

Again, it is given to none other than Samwise Gamgee to discover the necessity of living according to the right Story if we are to have real hope. In the Tower of Cirith Ungol, as he and Frodo have begun to doubt whether their Quest will ever succeed, Sam seeks to distinguish between tales that really matter and those that do not. There are many competing stories that vie for our loyalty, and Sam is trying to distinguish them, to locate the one hope-giving Story:

"We shouldn't be here at all," [Sam says to Frodo], "if we'd known more about it before we started. But I suppose it's often that way. The brave things in the old tales and songs, Mr. Frodo: adventures, as I used to call them. I used to think that they were things the wonderful folk of the stories went out and looked for, because they wanted them, because they were exciting and life was a bit dull, a kind of sport, as you might say. But that's not the way of it with the tales that really mattered, or the ones that stay in the mind. Folk seem to have been just landed in them, usually—their paths were laid that way, as you put it. But I expect they had lots of chances, like us, of turning back, only they didn't. And if they had, we shouldn't know, because they'd have been forgotten. We hear about those as just went on—and not all to a good end, mind you; at least not to what folk inside a story and not outside it call a good end. You know, coming home, and finding things all right, though not quite the same—like old Mr. Bilbo. But those aren't always the best tales to hear, though they may be the best tales to get landed in! I wonder what sort of tale we've fallen into?" (2.320–21)

Already Sam has discerned the crucial divide. On the one hand, the tales that do not matter concern there-and-back-again adventures—escapades undertaken because we are bored and thus seek excitement and entertainment. The tales that rivet the mind, on the other hand, involve a Quest that we do not choose for ourselves. Instead, we find ourselves embarked upon a journey or mission quite apart from our choosing. What counts, says Sam, is not whether the Quest succeeds but whether we turn back or slog ahead. One reason for not giving up, not quitting, is that the great tales are told about those who refused to surrender—those who ventured forward in hope.

As long as we are inside a Quest, Sam adds, we assume that it's a good one only if it has a good ending. But once we are outside it, we discover that perhaps the best stories do not have cheerful conclusions. Real heroism, Sam implies, requires us to struggle with hope, yet without the assurance of victory. Good endings may signal a too-easy victory that does not deepen our souls, while an unhappy conclusion reached nobly may be the mark of real character. Frodo interjects the idea that it's best not to know whether we are acting out a happy tale or a sad one. If we were assured of a happy destiny, then we would become presumptuous and complacent; if a sad one, then cynical and despairing. In neither case would we live and struggle by means of real hope.

Sam notes that Galadriel's star-glass, made with the light of the original Silmarils, involves them not in their own tale alone, but in a much larger one. "Don't the great tales ever end?" he asks. Frodo answers wisely in the negative. Each individual story—even the story of other fellowships and companies—is sure to end. But when our own story is done, he adds, someone else will take the one great tale forward to either a better or worse moment in its ongoing drama. What matters, Sam wisely concludes, is that we enact our proper role in an infinitely larger Story than our own little narrative:

"Things done and over and made into part of the great tales are different. Why, even Gollum might be good in a tale" (2.322).

Sam has here plumbed the depths of real hope. The "great tales" stand apart from mere adventures because they belong to the One Great Story. It is a story not only of those who fight heroically against evil, but also of those who are unwilling to exterminate such an enemy as Gollum. As Sam discerns, this Tale finds a surprising place even for evil. For it is not only the story of the stolen Silmarils and the destruction of the Ruling Ring, but the saga of Ilúvatar's entire cosmos—the narrative that moves from Creation through Calamity, on to Counter-Action, and finally to Correction and Consummation. To complete such a Quest requires the highest of all virtues: hope as well as faith working through *love* (Gal. 5:6).

The Love That Forgives

Hope and faith shall eventually pass away, but love shall abide forever. In Paradise there will be no need for faith, because God will be directly known. Neither shall there be any need for hope, for all that has been rightly yearned and longed for shall be fulfilled. Love alone will last unendingly because it unites us both with God and everyone else. Indeed, it defines who God is and who we are meant to be. Love as a theological virtue is not a natural human capacity, not a product of human willing and striving even at their highest. Because charity constitutes the triune God's own essence, it is always a gift and thus also a command.

About this matter as about so much else, Christians and Jews are fundamentally agreed. There is no Old Testament God of wrath set over against a New Testament God of love. Quite to the contrary, there is but a single covenant of the one God given to his people Israel and renewed in his son Jesus Christ. The *shema* calls Israel to love God in order to keep his commandments: "Hear, O Israel: The LORD our God is one LORD; and you shall love the LORD your God with all your heart, and with all your soul, and with all your might" (Deut. 6:4–5). When Jesus adds his own corollary to this first and greatest commandment, he derives it from the Old Testa-

ment: "you shall love your neighbor as yourself: I am the LORD"
(Lev. 19:18). The very character of God is mercy:

> The LORD is merciful and gracious, slow to anger and abound-
> ing in steadfast love. He will not always chide, nor will he keep
> his anger for ever. He does not deal with us according to our
> sins, nor requite us according to our iniquities. For as the heav-
> ens are high above the earth, so great is his steadfast love toward
> those who fear him; as far as the east is from the west, so far
> does he remove our transgressions from us. As a father pities his
> children, so the LORD pities those who fear him. For he knows
> our frame; he remembers that we are dust. (Ps. 103:8–14)

In both Testaments, the heart of God's love—and thus the real
impetus for human love—is forgiveness. Repeatedly Yahweh
refuses to destroy his unfaithful people, to break his covenant that
they have repeatedly violated. The prophet Hosea complains to
Yahweh about his wayward and wanton wife, and yet the Holy One
abjures Hosea to buy back—to redeem—his harlot spouse. So has
Israel played the prostitute to Yahweh, lusting after false gods. Yet
the Lord refuses to divorce his faithless people: "And I will make
for you a covenant on that day. . . . And I will betroth you to me for
ever; I will betroth you to me in righteousness and in justice, in
steadfast love, and in mercy" (Hos. 2:18–19). The supreme love
command in the New Testament is found in Jesus' charge to his followers that they forgive their enemies: "You have heard that it was
said, 'You shall love your neighbor and hate your enemy.' But I say
to you, Love your enemies and pray for those who persecute you"
(Matt. 5:43–44). Such love is possible only because God has had
mercy on us who are his real adversaries, on us who have slain his
Son: "But God shows his love for us in that while we were yet sin-
ners Christ died for us. . . . [W]hile we were enemies we were reconciled to God" (Rom. 5:8, 10). Thus is God himself called "the
Father of mercies" (2 Cor. 1:3).

Nowhere is *The Lord of the Rings* made more manifestly Christian than in its privileging of pity—mercy and forgiveness—as its
central virtue. The summons to pity is voiced most clearly by Gandalf after Frodo expresses his outrage that Bilbo had the chance to

kill the wicked Gollum but did not. Frodo has cause for his fury. Gollum was in fact seeking to slay Bilbo, and had Bilbo not put on the Ring to escape him, there is little doubt that Gollum would have succeeded in murdering Frodo's kinsman. Why, asks Frodo, should Bilbo have not given Gollum the justice he so fully deserved? Gandalf answers with a speech that lies at the moral and religious center of the entire epic:

> "What a pity that Bilbo did not stab that vile creature, [Frodo declares,] when he had a chance!"
> "Pity? [Gandalf replies.] It was Pity that stayed his hand. Pity, and Mercy: not to strike without need. And he has been well rewarded, Frodo. Be sure that [Bilbo] took so little hurt from the evil, and escaped in the end, because he began his ownership of the Ring so. With Pity."
> "I am sorry," said Frodo. "But I am frightened; and I do not feel any pity for Gollum."
> "You have not seen him," Gandalf broke in.
> "No, and I don't want to," said Frodo. ". . . Now at any rate he is as bad as an Orc, and just an enemy. He deserves death."
> "Deserves it! I daresay he does. Many that live deserve death. And some that die deserve life. Can you give it to them? Then do not be too eager to deal out death in judgement. For even the very wise cannot see all ends. I have not much hope that Gollum can be cured before he dies, but there is a chance of it. And he is bound up with the fate of the Ring. My heart tells me that he has some part to play yet, for good or ill, before the end; and when that comes, the pity of Bilbo may rule the fate of many— yours not least." (1.68–69)

"The pity of Bilbo may rule the fate of many" is the only declaration to be repeated in all three volumes of *The Lord of the Rings*. It is indeed the leitmotiv of Tolkien's epic, its animating theme, its Christian epicenter as well as its circumference. Gandalf's prophecy is true in the literal sense, for the same vile Gollum whom Bilbo had spared long ago finally enables the Ring's destruction. The wizard's saying is also true in the spiritual sense. For in this speech Gandalf lays out a decidedly non-pagan notion of mercy. As a creature far more sinning than sinned against, Gollum deserves his misery. He has committed Cain's sin in acquiring the Ring, slaying his cousin and friend. Yet while the Ring extended Gollum's life by five centuries and enabled him endlessly to relish raw fish, it has also made him utterly wretched. Evil is its own worst torment—as Gandalf urges Frodo to notice: "You have not seen him."

There is still a deeper reason for Gandalf's insistence on pity. In response to Frodo's demand that Gollum be given justice, the wizard offers a profound reading of mercy—the one remedy to Gollum's desolate condition. If all died who deserved punishment, says Gandalf, perhaps none would live. Many perish, he adds, who are worthy of life, and yet who can restore them? Gandalf supplies the answer to his own rhetorical question: none. Be exceedingly chary, he warns Frodo, about judging others and sentencing them to death. Though Gandalf speaks here of literal death, there are other kinds of death—scorn, contempt, dismissal—that such judgment could render. Frodo is in danger, Gandalf sees, of committing the subtlest and deadliest of all sins—self-righteousness. "Judge not, that you be not judged. For with the judgment you pronounce you will be judged, and the measure you give will be the measure you get" (Matt. 7:1–2).

If Frodo assesses Gollum by any other standard than his own escape from well-deserved punishment—insisting that Gollum be given justice, when Frodo himself has been given grace—he is in dread danger of presumption. Neither hobbits nor humans, Tolkien suggests, can live by the bread of merit alone. Gollum is not to be executed, though he may well deserve death, precisely because he is a fellow sinner, a fallen creature of feeble frame, a comrade in the stuff of dust. Gandalf admits that there is not much hope for Gollum's return to the creaturely circle, but neither is there much hope for many others, perhaps not even for most. To deny them such hope, Gandalf concludes, is to deny it also to oneself.

Tolkien runs a risk of miscomprehension in having Gandalf extol pity rather than mercy. In our world, pity implies a degrading act of condescension, a patronizing good deed performed by someone in a superior position for the sake of someone presumably inferior. Tolkien the linguist knows, on the contrary, that pity is rooted in the Latin *pietas*. Far from disparaging the one who is given it, pity establishes the fundamental solidarity of giver and receiver. Pity understood as *pietas* entails responsibility, duty, devotion, kindness, tenderness, even loyalty. In commending Bilbo's pity for Gollum, therefore, Gandalf is urging Frodo to acknowledge his elemental kinship with "that vile creature."

Gandalf's discourse on pity also marks the huge distance between Tolkien's book and the heroic world that is its inspiration. Among most ancient and pagan cultures—like their modern counterparts—pity is not a virtue. The Greeks, for example, extend pity only to the pathetic, the helpless, those who are able to do little or nothing for themselves. When Aristotle says that the function of tragic drama is to arouse fear and pity, he refers to the fate of a character such as Oedipus. We are to fear that Oedipus's fate might somehow be ours, and we are to pity him for the ineluctable circumstances of his life, his unjust fate. But pity is never to be given to the unjust or the undeserving, for such mercy would deny them the justice that they surely merit. Mercy of this kind—the kind that is so central to biblical faith—would indeed be a vice.

According to the warrior ethic of the ancient North, the offering of pardon to enemies is unthinkable: they must be utterly defeated. For Tolkien the Christian, by contrast, love understood as mercy and pity is essential: "You have heard that it was said, 'You shall love your neighbor and hate your enemy.' But I say to you, Love your enemies and pray for those who persecute you. . . . For if you love those who love you, what reward have you?" (Matt. 5:43–44, 46). Here we see the crucial distinction between *philia* as the love of friends who share our deepest concerns and *agape* as the love of those who are not only radically "other" to us, but who deserve our scorn and cannot reciprocate our pardon. We can make friends only with those whose convictions we share, but we are called to have pity for those whom we do not trust, even our enemies.

It is precisely such pity that Gandalf offers to Saruman after the battle of Helm's Deep. As we have seen, Saruman rejects it in the most vehement and scornful terms. Having at last learned Gandalf's central teaching, Frodo offers pardon to Saruman one last time—after the Ring has been destroyed and the hobbits are scouring the Shire of the evils that have been visited on it by Saruman and his thugs. Once Saruman is captured, there is a clamor that he be killed. In fact, Saruman courts his own execution by mocking his captors. But Frodo will have none of it: "I will not have him slain. It is useless to meet revenge with revenge: it will heal nothing" (3.298). Instead of receiving such mercy gladly, Saruman seeks to stab Frodo. Though Sam is ready to give Saruman the final sword thrust, Frodo again denies the villain the justice that he is due. He will not deal out judgment in death, knowing that, if Saruman dies in such rage, his life as a wizard will have indeed come to nothing—and perhaps worse than nothing:

> "No, Sam!" said Frodo. "Do not kill him even now. For he has not hurt me. And in any case I do not wish him to be slain in this evil mood. He was great once, of a noble kind that we should not dare to raise our hands against. He is fallen, and his cure is beyond us; but I would still spare him, in the hope that he may find it." (3.299)

Then follows one of the most revealing scenes in the entire epic. Instead of receiving this second grant of pity, Saruman is rendered furious by it. He knows that, in showing him pity, Frodo has removed the wizard's very reason for being. Frodo's pardon robs Saruman of his delicious self-pity, his self-justifying resentment, his self-sustaining fury. Having come to batten on his wrath, Saruman flings Frodo's pity back at him in a sputter of acrimony: "You have grown, Halfling," he said. "Yes, you have grown very much. You are wise, and cruel. You have robbed my revenge of sweetness, and now I must go hence in bitterness, in debt to your mercy. I hate it and you!" (3.299).

While revenge curdles the soul and paralyzes the will, pity frees those who will receive it. Repentance does not produce forgiveness, Tolkien shows, but rather the other way around: mercy enables contrition. This is made especially evident when Aragorn orders the assault on the Black Gate of Mordor. He knows that many of his troops are incapable of facing the Sauronic evil: "So desolate were those places and so deep the horror that lay on them that some of the host [the army of the Free Peoples] were unmanned, and they could neither walk nor ride further north." Rather than scorning their fear at having to fight "like men in a hideous dream made true," Aragorn has pity on them. He urges them to turn back with honor and dignity, not running but walking, seeking to find some other task that might aid the war against Sauron. Aragorn's mercy has a stunning effect. In some of the warriors, it overcomes their fear and enables them to rejoin the fray. Others take hope from Aragorn's pardon, encouraged to hear that there is "a manful deed within their measure" (3.162). And so they depart in peace rather than shame. This is the pity that Saruman bitterly rejected, for it would have called him out of his cowardly hatred and sweet revenge into a life of service and virtue.

Perhaps the most poignant scene of pardon in *The Lord of the Rings* occurs with the death of Boromir. He would seem to be the Judas of the story, for it is he who breaks the Fellowship by trying to seize the Ring from Frodo. Frodo in turn is forced to wear it in order to escape—not the orcs or the Ringwraiths or even Saruman, but Boromir his friend and fellow member of the Company. But no sooner has Boromir seen the horror that he has committed than he recognizes and repents of it: "What have I done? Frodo, Frodo!" he called. "Come back! A madness took me, but it has passed" (1.416). It is too late in the literal sense, because Frodo has already fled. But it is not too late for Boromir's redemption. He makes good on his solitary confession of sin by fighting orcs until they finally overcome him.

When Aragorn and Legolas and Gimli at last hear the horn of the desperate Boromir, they run to him, only to find him dying. Boromir does not boast of his valor in death, nor does Aragorn accuse him of evil. Perhaps because he can discern Aragorn's forgiving spirit, Boromir admits his sin, as if the future king were also a priest hearing his last confession: "I tried to take the Ring from Frodo," he said. "I am sorry. I have paid" (2.16). Boromir does not mean that he has recompensed for his dreadful attempt to seize the Ring. He means that he has paid the terrible price of breaking trust with Frodo. In almost his last breath, therefore, Boromir confesses that he has failed.

Aragorn will not let Boromir die in the conviction that his whole life has been ruined by a momentary act of madness—even though it was prompted by Boromir's arrogant confidence in his own courage. Rather than pointing to his terrible guilt in betraying Frodo and the Company, Aragorn absolves the dying hero by emphasizing the real penance Boromir has performed in fighting evil to the end, even when no one was present to witness his deed: "'No!' said Aragorn, taking his hand and kissing his brow. 'You have conquered. Few have gained such a victory. Be at peace!'" (2.16). We know that Boromir has received his pardon, for his last gesture is a smile. To confirm Boromir's nobility in both life and death, Aragorn, Legolas, and Gimli give Boromir a reverent ceremonial funeral by placing his body on a boat and setting him afloat toward the sea. Many miles away, but at the same hour, Faramir experienced a mystical vision of his brother's sea burial and ultimate fate. Faramir saw that, for all his vainglory, Boromir ended in a state of grace: "Whether he erred or no, of this I am sure: he died well, achieving some good thing. His face was more beautiful even than in life" (2.278).

"So faith, hope, love abide, these three; but the greatest of these is love" (1 Cor. 13:13). Paul is not offering any sort of paean to human love as having its origin and end in our own powers. Tolkien captures the transcendent, even divine quality of real love by having it issue in a pity and pardon utterly unknown either to the warrior cultures of the ancient world or to our own equally merciless culture of competition. "The pity of Bilbo may rule the fate of many" is not, therefore, a motto meant only for Middle-earth. It is the key to our own transformation as well.

Chapter Five

Consummation:
When Middle-earth Shall Be Unmarred

*O*ne of the enduring enigmas left by the conclusion to the *The Lord of the Rings* is how to deal with its surpassing sadness. The breakup of the Fellowship is somber enough, but the departure of Frodo and Gandalf for the Grey Havens is veritably tearful. Frodo is too worn and wearied by the spiritual terrors that come from having borne the Ring ever to enjoy the fruits of the Company's accomplished errand. Gandalf, in turn, must also leave his companions because he has given them his maximum wisdom and guidance, and because the Third Age of elves and wizards is now ended. The book is over, and yet readers want to the story to continue. We can find considerable solace in Sam Gamgee's immense moral growth, especially since Frodo predicts that he will become the mayor of Hobbiton. Yet the long-term prospects for Middle-earth hardly seem to give cause for rejoicing. The occasional references to "when the world will be changed" are only vaguely hopeful, and nothing distinctively Christian can be garnered from them.

Why, then, is the history of Middle-earth not caught in an endlessly downward spiral toward final defeat and death? Why, if in the end Arda itself will be destroyed and Valinor with it, is there not cause to despair? Why, in the meantime, does the Fourth Age of Men not promise a future altogether as disconsolate as the mortalism—where Chaos and Unreason finally triumph—of both ancient and modern paganism? Of all the Free Peoples in Middle-earth, our own species has acquitted itself perhaps least well. Melkor's seductions have proved ever so fatal to our humankind, especially given our fear of death and the many temptations that this dread of dying brings with it. Why, given such a dispiriting forecast about the human future of Middle-earth, should Tolkien not be charged with an abiding antimodernism, and with a bilious misanthropy as well: a fundamental contempt for his own human race?

The answer lies in what Christopher Tolkien called a "very remarkable and hitherto unknown work" (MR, 303), "The Debate of Finrod and Andreth." Perhaps written in the late 1950s, it contains a stunning prophecy of Ilúvatar's own eventual entry into Middle-earth history. Such an Incarnation is devoutly to be wished, for it would thereby link Tolkien's imaginative world with Christian revelation in an explicit way. It would also reveal the real hope that Tolkien holds out for the Age of Men that dawns at the ending of *The Lord of the Rings*. And as we have noticed throughout this study, hope for Middle-earth's hobbits and men—who are both creatures of our own kind—is always hope for us as well.

It is important to follow the exchange between Andreth and Finrod, for it reveals a great deal about Tolkien's understanding of death—whether it is natural or unnatural for death to mark the end of human life, and whether our souls are separable from our bodies. Finrod is the wisest of the Noldor elves, and Andreth is a woman similarly steeped in the lore and history and wisdom of Men. They debate the nature of mortality and what might lie beyond it. Finrod makes the standard elven argument that men have brief lives because mortality seems to be their unique gift from Ilúvatar.

There is reason to believe that Tolkien himself at least partially shared this view. As we have seen over again, death comes as an authentic blessing to the fallen human race. To live forever would be to suffer an everlasting life of either presumption or despair. In the elvish view, death is the natural end of human and hobbitic existence, and it would not strike terror if we were not rebels against Ilúvatar. "*Death*," argues Finrod, "is but the name that we give to something that [Melkor] has tainted, and it sounds therefore evil; but untainted its name would be good" (MR, 310).

Andreth vigorously disputes Finrod's case. She contends that Men were not born for death because it does not belong to our nature. We have become short-lived, she insists, only "through the malice of the Lord of the Darkness whom [men] do not name" (MR, 309). In her view, we rightly dread death because it is indeed the real enemy. The elves cannot understand the evil of death, she contends, because their species does not experience it, except in unusual instances—through grief or accident. "To you [death] may be in pain, it may be bitter and a loss—but only for a time. . . . For ye know that in dying you do not leave the world, and that you may return to life [in Valinor]" (MR, 311). For men, by contrast, death tracks us down like a hunter slaying its prey. And in Middle-earth as we now know it, nothing lies beyond death but oblivion:

> Be a Man strong, or swift, or bold; be he wise or a fool; be he evil, or be he in all the deeds of his days just and merciful, let him love the world or loathe it, he must die and must leave it—and become carrion that men are fain to hide or to burn. (MR, 311)

Here the debate takes a decisive turn, as Andreth begins to make her case that, in the beginning, Men were not in fact created in order to die, but rather were *"born to life everlasting, without any shadow of any end"* (MR, 314). This remarkable claim does not catch Finrod entirely by surprise. He confesses that elves have often noted a strange human characteristic: whereas the elves are thoroughly at home in the world, men are not. Men seem to have a memory of some other life, some other world, from which they have become alienated and estranged, but to which they seek a return. "The Eldar [elves] say of Men," Finrod observes, "that they look at no thing for itself; that if they study it, it is to discover something else; that if they love it, it is only (so it seems) because it reminds them of some other dearer thing" (MR, 316).

Thus far, Finrod and Ardeth would seem to be agreeing with the standard Platonic argument that humans have a deep longing for a Life beyond life because they have sprung from an eternal world. Behind the shadow of this mortal life lies the true Life. Having come from another realm, according to this view, Men are meant to return to it, whether by dying or by finding a kind of eternity within mortal existence itself. From Plato through much of medieval thought on to Wordsworth and C. S. Lewis, this idea of immortality has often held sway among Christians and non-Christians alike.

Precisely at this point Andreth's argument takes a radically non-Platonic turn. She argues, on the contrary, that man is not a body (hröa) containing a mind or a soul (fëa). The soul is not boxed in the body as if it were a ghost in a machine. For if this were the case, then death would contain no real terror, since it would enable men gladly to shed their mortal existence in favor of the immortal. On the contrary, our bodies are essential to our souls and minds. A better analogy, says Andreth, is to envision the mind-soul as the Dweller while the body is the House—each being essential to the other. The House that the Dwellers build and inhabit would have no purpose without them. The Dwellers, in turn, would have no life apart from the place wherein they dwell. In which case, she adds, the severance of the body and soul in death is a dread event—indeed a calamity caused by Melkor, not Ilúvatar. The bodies and souls of men are meant to be united forever in a living and caring harmony:

> For were it "natural" for the body to be abandoned and die, but "natural" for the fëa to live on, then there would indeed be a disharmony in Man, and his parts would not be united by love. His body would be a hindrance at best, or a chain. An imposition indeed, not a gift.
> . . . I hold that in this we are as ye [elves] are, truly Incarnates, and that we do not live in our right being and its fullness save in a union of love and peace between the House and the Dweller. Wherefore death, which divides them, is a disaster to both. (MR, 317)

Here Tolkien enables Andreth to remain profoundly faithful to both the Bible and Christian tradition. Genesis's second creation account envisions our humanity as an inseparable unity of body and soul, with death coming as an utterly unnatural intrusion into God's good creation, once Adam and Eve eat the forbidden fruit. So in the New Testament as well is death explicitly called "the last enemy to be destroyed" (1 Cor. 15:26). The all-important Christian doctrine of the resurrection of the body also confirms Andreth's case that we have no souls that exist somehow apart from our bodies, but that we are an indissoluble union of the two. Neither is meant to tyrannize the other; rather are both to be joined in joy and peace.

The human longing that elves have noticed to persist in men, it follows, is not a desire for some other world than this one. It is, instead, a yearning for a return to the harmony and unity between body and soul that were lost when men became rebels against Ilúvatar. Melkor brought death into the world as his means of sundering the spirits and bodies of men from their intended unity. This, then, is the real calamity called "Arda Marred" (MR, 318).

Here both Finrod and Ardeth begin to discern the answer to the riddle that has vexed many, perhaps most, of Tolkien's readers: why does the Age of Men not mark a sure decline from the wondrous era of elves and wizards? The answer is that, unlike either wizards or elves, men were created by Ilúvatar to cure the death curse wrought by Melkor. The original errand of Men, Ardeth insists, is to serve "as agents of the magnificence of Eru: to enlarge the Music and surpass the Vision of the World" given originally by Ilúvatar to the valar (MR, 318).

Only men can reunite what Melkor divided in death because they alone, among Ilúvatar's creatures, have souls that can virtually divinize their bodies and thus keep them in perpetual undying life. As Aquinas taught, the souls of men give their bodies their true form, their real existence. Thus could the right kind of man restore the lost body-soul harmony that afflicts men and elves alike:

> [T]he *fëa* when it departs must take with it the *hröa*. And what can this mean unless it be that the *fëa* shall have the power to uplift the *hröa*, as its eternal spouse and companion, into an endurance everlasting beyond Eä, and beyond Time? Thus would Arda, or part thereof, be healed not only of the taint of Melkor, but released even from the limits that were set for it in the "Vision of Eru" of which the Valar speak. (MR, 318)

Now at last Ardeth brings her argument to its culmination. If men were originally created for the healing of the marred earth, and if this Arda Remade would deliver even the elves themselves from the gradual fading away of their bodies, as well as their final destruction at the End of Arda, what new kind of man could possibly overcome the curse of Melkor called permanent death? There is but a single answer, Ardeth replies, a single "Old Hope" that was held by men of ancient times—that *Ilúvatar himself should take on earthly life, that the Author of the cosmic drama should become its lead Actor*: "they say that the One will himself enter into Arda, and heal Men and all the Marring from the beginning to the end" (MR, 321).

This Tolkienian prophecy of the incarnation of God in Middle-earth is deeply Christian. Just as the new life wrought in Israel and Christ is immeasurably greater than the old life lost in Adam and Eve, so will Arda Healed not be simply old Arda renovated: it will be a radically new and transformed world—"a third thing and a greater, and yet the same" (MR, 318), "something new, richer than the 'first design'" (MR, 333). Thus will the ancient enigma of evil at last be answered, since Morgoth's disharmony shall contribute, albeit unintentionally, to the final harmony of Ilúvatar's grand symphonic work. Middle-earth will discover the profound truth of Eru's declaration that a "beauty not before conceived [shall] be brought into Eä, and *evil yet be good to have been*" (S, 98; emphasis added). Nor will Ilúvatar, in order to become incarnate, be required to invade the world as a stranger and alien, since his Flame Imperishable already permeates all things as their living spirit. As Finrod observes, "He is already in it, as well as outside. . . . But indeed the 'in-dwelling' and the 'out-living' are not in the same mode" (MR, 322). When Eru enters Arda to defeat Melkor and to bring the cosmic Drama to its completion, Tolkien explains in a note, the One will do so in a way that preserves both his immanence and his transcendence:

> Eru could not enter *wholly* into the world and its history, which is, however great, only a finite Drama. He must as Author always remain "outside" the Drama, even though that Drama depends on His design and His will for its beginning and continuance, in every detail and moment. Finrod therefore thinks that He will, when He comes, have to be both "outside" and inside. (MR, 335)

Tolkien here affirms—albeit in distinctively mythical terms—the central Christian claim that the Incarnation is not a violation of human dignity but its wondrous fulfillment and completion. In the rabbi of Nazareth "the whole fulness of deity dwells bodily" (Col. 2:9). God is at once "inside" and "outside" Jesus Christ—inside as the incarnate Second Person of the Trinity, outside as the Heavenly Father who directs the cosmic drama. Hence the Christian claim that Jesus Christ alone is *vere homo, vere deus*—true God and true Man. Hence also Tolkien's claim that the enfleshment of Ilúvatar will occur in Middle-earth precisely as it has occurred in human history.

It is not alien to the spirit of *The Lord of the Rings* to conclude this study by speculating about the form that the Incarnation might take in Arda. In what era of Middle-earth history and in what kind of creature would Eru become earthly? Would the One await the dawning of a glorious Age of Men and there incarnate himself in an Aragorn-like figure? We know from Tolkien's aborted story called "The New Shadow" that the era introduced by the kingship of Aragorn did not bring a long-lived splendor. For while Gondor and Arnor were restored to something akin to their former greatness, the grandeur did not last. Within a hundred years of Mordor's downfall and Aragorn's death, a New Shadow had arisen. The old darkness descended afresh because the citizens of Gondor became complacent, self-satisfied, and restless—bored with the triumph of "peace, justice and prosperity" (L, 344). Satanistic cults arose, says Tolkien, and orc games flourished among adolescents (L, 419).

It takes no great originality of mind or imagination to discern the analogies between such evil mythological times and the world of either first-century Palestine or twenty-first-century Europe and America. Yet we must assume that in precisely such a degraded and decadent world would Ilúvatar become incarnate. Whether he is called Eru or God, the Lord of all things did not take on human form in the midst of a splendid civilization at its apex—lest he be worshiped as yet another triumphant earth-deity. Rather did he enter history in a nation dwelling at the edge of the Roman empire, and among a people who were negligible by nearly every worldly measure. Even among the Jews, the triune God did not assume the life of a ruler or king, a prophet or philosopher, but rather the role of a servant: "Christ Jesus, . . . though he was in the form of God, did not count equality with God a thing to be grasped, but emptied himself, taking the form of a servant, being born in the likeness of men. And being found in human form he humbled himself and became obedient unto death, even death on a cross" (Phil. 2:5–8).

To be a servant is to be liberated from self-concern. It is to be so fully devoted to the common good that one hardly thinks of one's own wants and needs at all. Such self-giving commonality is the essence of life in the Shire, and it is surely the chief reason the hobbits are entrusted with destroying the Ring. Like others of their kind, Frodo and Sam, as well as Merry and Pippin, can be trusted to fulfill so immense a task as the unmaking of the Ring because they live contentedly, not always yearning for a grander life. Their virtue is not that they are small-minded but that they truly love and serve each other. They care little or nothing about accruing either power or wealth. Even in battle, they refuse to deal in grand abstractions, crying out, instead, "The Shire!"

The close kinship between the Gospel and the central call of the Quest is not far to find. Jesus commands his disciples not to save their lives for their own sake but to lose them for his sake and the Kingdom. "For what does it profit a man, to gain the whole world and forfeit his life? For what can a man give in return for his life?" (Mark 8:36–37). By the end of the Quest, the entire Fellowship has learned this most basic but also profoundest of all lessons. Even Sam knew from the beginning that he was not following Frodo merely to see elves and mountains and dragons. He was undertaking an errand that would require nothing less than everything. "I know we are going to take a very long road, into darkness; but I know I can't turn back. . . . I don't rightly know what I want: but I have something to do before the end, and it lies ahead, not in the Shire. I must see it through, sir," he says to Frodo, "if you understand me" (1.96). Such, simply put, is the meaning of servanthood in the Kingdom.

So has Bilbo taken little hurt from his many uses of the Ring because he had mercy on Gollum and because he thought so little about its potential benefits for himself. Gollum, by contrast, reveals precisely what a servant is not; he cares only for himself, speaking always of the Ring as "My Precious." Sam Gamgee is the ultimate hero of *The Lord of the Rings* because he is the ultimate servant. That he wants nothing other than to serve his master Frodo makes him, if not the greatest of all the hobbits, certainly the most admirable. "Whoever would be great among you must be your servant, and whoever would be first among you must be slave of all. For the Son of man also came not to be served but to serve, and to give his life as a ransom for many" (Mark 10:43–45).

It is neither idle nor fantastic, I believe, to imagine Ilúvatar entering Arda in the form of a hobbit. The average Jew of Jesus' day was perhaps little if any larger than Tolkien's hobbits. Yet it is the size of their souls rather than their bodies that matters. For it is from such hobbit-souls that the Kingdom of God is truly made— whether we are considering the Lord and Savior who enfleshes the triune God, or whether we are numbering his lowliest disciples. Elrond the Elflord saw this truth from the beginning, when he not only appointed the members of the Fellowship but also explained the astonishing nature of their mission: "This quest may be attempted by the weak with as much hope as the strong. Yet such is oft the course of deeds that move the wheels of the world: small hands do them because they must, while the eyes of the great are elsewhere" (1.283).

In the world of Middle-earth, the Consummation of All Things occurs neither with the fall of Mordor nor the coronation of Aragorn, but with the coming incarnation of Ilúvatar. The One who orders the life of Eä and Arda, I have argued, may well take the form of a hobbit—just as God's own incarnation occurred in a humble Jewish servant. For only in such divine lowliness can Arda be unmarred. In our own world, the Kingdom still arrives through this strange strength to be found in self-surrender. "The weakness of God is stronger than men" (1 Cor. 1:25), Paul declares, for Christ has assured him that his "power is made perfect in weakness" (2 Cor. 12:9). So it is with Frodo, as he explains to Sam why he cannot return to Hobbiton at the end of the Quest. Frodo takes no credit for rescuing his region from Sauron's evil. In fact, his verbs shift from the active to the passive voice—from declaring that he has done his best to save the Shire, suffering wounds that no hobbitic medicine can heal, to confessing that the Shire has been saved even when his best did not suffice: "I have been too deeply hurt, Sam. I tried to save the Shire, and it has been saved, but not for me. It must often be so, Sam, when things are in danger: some one has to give them up, lose them, so that others may keep them" (3.309).

The urgent call of the gospel is precisely the summons to give up even good things, to surrender all coercive power, to lose one's own life in order that others might find the treasure of the Kingdom. This coming reign of God beyond the walls of the world will be completed only with the return of the servant-king who has already inaugurated his Kingdom by losing his own life and by creating a community of the faithful who will also lose theirs. As the people of God in the world, the church is empowered by the Spirit who makes the crucified and risen Lord present, even as it eagerly awaits his final consummation of all things, when there shall be a new heaven and a new earth.

Far from dreading the appointed end, Christians work confidently in the task of unmarring the earth. One of our best guides for this high and holy vocation is the work of J. R. R. Tolkien, especially *The Lord of the Rings*. It began in 1930 or 1931 when—perhaps bored with grading tedious student exams—Tolkien penned a sentence that had entered his mind uncannily and unbidden: "In a hole in the ground there lived a hobbit." From that modest beginning we have come to our own similarly modest conclusion: Christians are called to be hobbit-like servants of the King and his Kingdom. Frodo and Sam are first in the reign of Ilúvatar because they are willing to be last and least among those who "move the wheels of the world."

Bibliography

Works by J. R. R. Tolkien

The Fellowship of the Ring. 2d ed. Boston: Houghton Mifflin, 1967.
The History of Middle-earth. Vol. 10, *Morgoth's Ring: The Later Silmarillion.* Part 1, *The Legends of Aman.* Edited by Christopher Tolkien. Boston: Houghton Mifflin, 1993.
The Hobbit. Boston: Houghton Mifflin, 1978.
The Letters of J. R. R. Tolkien. Edited by Humphrey Carpenter. Boston: Houghton Mifflin, 1981.
"The Monsters and the Critics" and Other Essays. Edited by Christopher Tolkien. Boston: Houghton Mifflin, 1984.
The Peoples of Middle-earth. Edited by Christopher Tolkien. Boston: Houghton Mifflin, 1996.
The Return of the King. 2d ed. Boston: Houghton Mifflin, 1967.
The Silmarillion. Boston: Houghton Mifflin, 1977.
Smith of Wootton Major. Illustrated by Pauline Baynes. Boston: Houghton Mifflin, 1978.
The Two Towers. 2d ed. Boston: Houghton Mifflin, 1965.

Related Works

Birzer, Bradley. *J. R. R. Tolkien's Sanctifying Myth: Understanding Middle-earth.* Wilmington, Del.: Intercollegiate Studies Institute, 2002.
Carpenter, Humphrey. *J. R. R. Tolkien: A Biography.* Boston: Houghton Mifflin, 1977.
Chance, Jane. *Tolkien's Art: "A Mythology for England."* London: Macmillan, 1979.
Duriez, Colin. *Tolkien and* The Lord of the Rings*: A Guide to Middle-earth.* Mahwah, N.J.: HiddenSpring, 2001.
Foster, Robert. *The Complete Guide to Middle-earth: From* The Hobbit *to* The Silmarillion. New York: Ballantine, 1978.

Isaacs, Neil D., and Rose A. Zimbardo. *Tolkien and the Critics: Essays on J. R. R. Tolkien's* The Lord of the Rings. Notre Dame, Ind.: University of Notre Dame, 1968.

Kocher, Paul. *The Master of Middle-earth: The Fiction of J. R. R. Tolkien.* Boston: Houghton Mifflin, 1972.

MacIntyre, Alasdair. *After Virtue: A Study in Moral Theory.* 2d ed. Notre Dame, Ind.: University of Notre Dame, 1984.

Meilaender, Gilbert C. *The Theory and Practice of Virtue.* Notre Dame, Ind.: University of Notre Dame, 1984.

Pearce, Joseph. *Tolkien: A Celebration: Collected Writings on a Literary Legacy.* San Francisco: Ignatius, 1999.

Pieper, Josef. *The Four Cardinal Virtues: Prudence, Justice, Fortitude, Temperance.* Translated by Richard and Clara Winston, et al. Notre Dame, Ind.: University of Notre Dame, 1966.

Purtill, Richard. *J. R. R. Tolkien: Myth, Morality, and Religion.* New ed. San Francisco: Ignatius Press, 2003.

Shippey, Tom. *J. R. R. Tolkien: Author of the Century.* Boston: Houghton Mifflin, 2001.

Wadell, Paul J. *Friendship and the Moral Life.* Notre Dame, Ind.: University of Notre Dame, 1989.

Acknowledgments

CPSIA information can be obtained
at www.ICGtesting.com
Printed in the USA
FFOW03n1658051217
43805190-42734FF

9 780664 226107